The Science of Emotional Resilience:

Find Balance and Strength, Become Unbreakable, and Overcome Adversity

By Peter Hollins,
Author and Researcher at petehollins.com

Table of Contents

Introduction

Though I wasn't the best student in school, I was able to develop a close friendship with my high school English teacher, Mr. Locke.

I'm not sure why he took an interest in me, but I suppose the narrative to be told is that's how I ended up as a writer, and I have him to thank for all of it. Unfortunately, that would be false to say, and it's not remotely what we talked about most of the time.

Throughout the whole year, he was fun to ask about the books we were reading for class and what he actually thought about them. However, things got really interesting when the end of the year drew close, and he started to open up about the people in my class—my peers. Of course, this was a dream come true for me: an adult willing to gossip with me about my fellow students?

Looking back, this was wildly inappropriate for Mr. Locke to engage in such topics, but it's not like the teachers weren't doing it among themselves, anyway.

He didn't have a reputation as an easy teacher, and he was known to be fair. He let me in on a little secret of his: whenever he had to give negative feedback, he would always make sure to try to build up the individual student a couple of days before. He would do this to make sure their self-esteem, at least in the realm of his class, was sufficiently high, such that his negative feedback wouldn't have as big of an impact. He wanted students to not take things so personally, and be able to separate his comments on their work from them as a person. He wanted them to hear "This paper could use work," not "You need work."

My teenage mind was blown away, and I told him that he was so clever to use "Jedi mind tricks" on his students. He told me there were a few students he would do this on more than others because he felt they had low self-esteem, or he knew they were being bullied outside of his class. My adult mind still admires him and thinks that he had tremendous foresight into how people worked—especially future adults that were still figuring themselves out and who had fragile egos. It wasn't until much later that I realized he was helping students gain emotional resilience through raising their self-worth.

Self-esteem is an essential component of emotional resilience, and is often deemed *the immune system of emotions*. When it's high, you can handle what's thrown your way, and when it's low, you are more likely to collapse under scrutiny. Mr. Locke had somehow dialed into that and instilled that into his students.

Emotional resiliency is a trait that is like the background music in a movie. When it's there, you don't notice it and it seems that scenes just fit together without a hitch. However, if it's missing, suddenly words are taken the wrong way, everything feels wrong, and the scene falls apart. In other words, you notice it when you need it, but not when you don't.

Therein lies the conundrum of resiliency—how do you get it before you need it, and how do you know if you don't have it? The ugly truth is that none of us are naturally born with it. Some of us are put into nasty situations where we develop coping mechanisms for strength, but that doesn't mean you are resilient. It just means the dam hasn't broken yet.

It might be a scary realization, or an empowering one—*I've gotten this far without being truly resilient? Good things are ahead. It's all downhill from here.*

Not quite, but the hope for this book is to arm you, whoever you are and whatever you may or may not have suffered, with tools and techniques to persevere and thrive. Emotional resiliency is one of those rare qualities that causes a drastic shift in how you see the world. More importantly, it allows you to see *you* and gain better self-awareness of your thought patterns and behaviors. After all, it's tough to avoid walking into an emotional minefield if you see it only as a meadow.

Chapter 1. Our Volatile Emotions

Emotions are a major part of our existence and our identity as humans. Yet we don't often take a moment to think about where they come from, what they mean, why we feel certain ways, and how emotion actually affects us.

Why did I cry at that movie?
Because it was sad. But why cry?
Because that's what you do when you're sad.
But why?

We just accept that we are affected and don't take the time to think about how to strengthen or regulate certain emotions for greater well-being. Unfortunately, it's this lack of attention that leads precisely to a lack of resilience. If you don't understand the forces at work inside your brain, you can only but fall prey to them, with no hope of regulating or even combating them.

What are emotions and why do they affect us so?

This can fit as easily into a biology course as a philosophy course. For our purposes, we will try to address these questions from the former perspective: how do they function, what is their role, and why are they capable of completely dictating our lives?

Theories of Emotions

How do we even feel emotions? How do we know and understand what we feel and why we feel it?

If you were to ask 100 people to answer those questions, you would probably get 100 answers—even among scientists. Before diving into an exploration of the biological roots, however, it's worth exploring two of the most typical ways emotions are explained.

The first is called the *cognitive appraisal theory.*

This theory states that emotions are judgments about the extent that a current situation meets your expectations and goals, no matter how you define them. Happiness is felt because it is an evaluation that your expectations are being met or satisfied. If you win the lottery, you feel happiness because it solves your financial needs and likely exceeds your expectations. If you're asked out on a date, you feel happiness because it holds the promise of satisfying your romantic needs. In the same way, when you feel sadness, it is an evaluation that your goals are not being met, and anger might be the feeling that is aimed at whatever is blocking your goals.

Here, emotions are an instinctual reaction to objects or situations that relate to your expectations and goals. Often our goals are not clearly defined, as they can be both subconscious and conscious. You may not be able to say exactly why you're happy or disappointed at times—this theory sheds light on the fact that you subconsciously held some type of expectation that was or was not met.

If you are unemployed and presented with a job offer, you will feel happiness because you see it as a way to solve your financial worries. Alternatively, if you lose your job, you are saddened because you lose your financial stability. Your emotions are tied to how your status quo changes—another way we hold expectations we don't realize. In some cases, it may have little to do with the situation itself; maybe you've always hated your job and have always wanted to leave it. But when you're faced with the unexpected loss, you are saddened because it represents the loss of stability and your future career.

The cognitive appraisal theory speaks to your perception of how well a situation meets your goals and expectations, so your emotions will be a reflection of that. Understanding this theory means that you can better evaluate your emotions by always determining what they are oriented on. It essentially states that your emotions require something to revolve around.

This could seem overly simplistic, and indeed, it's mostly worth understanding as background for other, more-involved theories of emotion. It might serve as a good rule of thumb, however, and help you realize if you are holding subconscious expectations one way or another.

The second explanation of the nature of emotions is that they are more based in biology and science rather than in the psychological. In fact, that emotions are purely an interpretation of the body's signals.

Psychologists William James and Carl Lange proposed that emotions are just the perceptions of change in the physiology of your body. For example, changes in heart rate, breathing, perspiration, and hormone levels. This theory argues that emotions such as happiness are merely a physiological perception instead of a judgment as the previous theory states. Other emotions like sadness and anger are also mental reactions to different kinds of biological functions.

According to James and Lange, your body's state will change, which will spur you to associate an emotion with it. For example, imagine you are about to perform a speech in front of a group of people and think of your body's reaction beforehand. You might feel your heart pumping faster or your breathing increasing slightly. Your mind will associate the combination of these physical reactions with a feeling of nervousness.

There is undoubtedly a connection between emotions and physiological changes. However, the problem with this account is that bodily states are not nearly as fine-tuned or diverse as the many different kinds of emotions. Returning to the previous example, your heart pumping and increased breathing may also be interpreted as a feeling of excitement because of the close physiological similarities. This is the problem with associating emotions with physical reactions because you often have more emotions than reactions, and many biological responses are too similar to differentiate.

Understanding that emotions may be tied to your physical reactions means you may be able to convince yourself of alternative emotions. Imagine you are about to partake in some public speaking. Telling yourself that you are excited instead of nervous, considering the similarity in bodily reactions, may help you better face the task ahead of you. It can be quite beneficial to perceive negative physiological signs and use them for positive purposes.

Both of these theories aren't necessarily accurate or true, though they both seem quite logical. However, we will now move on to the true science and biology of emotions and how they function in the brain and body. After all, it's better to learn about how systems function first and then make a hypothesis, as opposed to merely making assumptions that seem logical at first glance.

This will help highlight why people would draw the conclusions they do about emotions and how the two theories above were formed, and how they aren't necessarily true.

What Are Emotions, Really?

Emotions, in the most general definition, are a neural impulse that moves you to act. They are something the brain commands to achieve a healthier existence, one that has evolved over time to help us survive and meet certain needs.

Psychologist Linda Davidoff defines emotion as a feeling that is expressed through physiological functions such as facial expressions, heartbeat, and certain behavior such as aggression, crying, or covering the face with hands. According to her, emotions would then be a result of changes in the brain, where neurochemicals such as dopamine, noradrenaline, and serotonin increase or lower the brain's activity level according to what is more beneficial in the circumstances.

For example, the human emotion of love is proposed to have evolved from circuits from the brain that were stimulated and designed for the care, feeding, and grooming of offspring. Having offspring around eventually cemented these pathways and associated it with positive, nurturing behavior.

Emotion makes us act a certain way based on the stimuli that we have processed, and is the interpretation of a series of physical changes. When you are in a situation where your palms begin to sweat, your heartbeat increases, and you are actively searching your surroundings, your body will do these physical things without much thought. They are reactive. But your mind will subsequently interpret the combination of these behavioral changes with a feeling of fear. First you have the stimuli, then the physical reactions, and then the psychological reaction—the emotion—that comes after.

It's important to note that often the brain is wrong, and the brain's concept of "beneficial" is not always compatible with the modern age.

When neurologists explored deeply the brain, they discovered that depression, love, kindness, aggression, abstract thinking, judgment, patience, instincts, and memories all have biochemical causes and even veritable physical locations. Because all of these feelings, emotions, and characteristics have foundations in the brain, this means that they can all be radically affected by brain damage and brain surgery.

There are several degenerative diseases of the brain that can erode personality. Brain damage can lead to sudden changes in character, tumors can alter our feelings, and biochemical imbalances can radically swing our mood.

One of the most famous examples of brain structure altering emotions and personality is the curious case of Phineas Gage. In 1848, a work explosion led to a metal pole going straight through Gage's skull. Despite the injury, he survived, albeit with an enormous hole in his skull and with a sizable part of his brain missing for the rest of his life. The damage to his frontal lobes caused a radical change in his personality and character. Prior to the accident, he was conscientious, upright, and respected. After the accident, he was suddenly abusive, profane, irritable, and irresponsible. He was simply a different person, unrecognizable to family and friends.

There was no other possible conclusion other than the areas that were destroyed regulated certain parts of the personality and certain emotions. Later, neurologists explained this more precisely, in that the brain's frontal lobes are associated with moderating impulsive behavior, setting goals, and other abstract areas of thought. Those around him described him as having become fitful, irreverent, prone to the "grossest profanity which was not previously his custom," and "a child in his intellectual capacity" but with "the animal passions of a strong man."

Gage's case was one of the first true revelations that proved that emotions originated from a biological source and were a direct result of the brain, instead of being associated with the soul, heart, or simple expectations.

Modern research indicates that during events, the sensory information that you pick up is transmitted to the thalamus, the relay center of the brain, before being transferred to the amygdala and the brain cortex. The amygdala instantly processes the information and sends signals so that hormones are released that activate the autonomic nervous system. Meanwhile, the brain cortex slowly processes the sensory information from the thalamus in the background, a slower system overall.

The amygdala causes a person's instantaneous response to an emotion-evoking event. There is no thought in this; it is pure instinct. The brain has evolved to have two different tracks of stimuli-processing: one quick and one slower. The quicker one is designed for protection and survival: when the amygdala thinks there is a threat that must be acted upon immediately in one way or another. Alternatively, the brain cortex is responsible for gradual processing, which allows someone to evaluate the emotion-evoking event, and even regulate their emotions surrounding it.

This fast and slow reaction is something that can be seen in everyday life, and is much simpler when seen first-hand. If there is a sound in the middle of the night that wakes you, you will instantly be alert and ready for action, even if you've had little sleep and your whole body is exhausted. This is an instinctual reaction to a threat so that you have chances at survival. This is something that can easily be traced back as a result of evolution. If you are slow to respond to threats, you will not be able to survive.

On the other hand, the slow processing of external stimuli in the brain cortex is for less-instinctual emotions. Something like love takes longer to process because of the number of contributing factors. It is not instinctual to feel love when presented with an event or situation. It takes a bit longer and more processing of the overall situation.

So what are emotions? We've discovered that they are part biological and part based on evaluating the world around us. But they are far more than that, as any romantic comedy will show you. Perhaps the best and most helpful way to conceive of emotions is this: they depend on your unique brain chemistry, your circumstances and status quo, your expectations, and your entire life of experiences that inform everything prior.

The Purpose of Emotions

The purpose of emotions really stems from that track of processing that goes directly to the amygdala for instant action.

They are one of the most important indicators of what will keep us alive and happy by letting us know what we should avoid and what we should pursue. Think of emotions as the mental version of your sense of taste. You will avoid foods that don't taste good, such as rotten fruit, because they are likely to be bad for you, and you will actively eat what tastes good to you because they are likely to be good for your health and survival—though not your waistline. Of course, this is why fat tastes amazing, and why feces have a foul smell.

Emotions go a level further than helping you avoid rotten fruit. They help you avoid dangerous situations, psychological damage, and less-subtle dangers that are just as fatal.

Emotions lead to the well-being and ultimate survival of both individuals and groups by providing a quick and automated reaction to certain events and circumstances. This is so that we can avoid danger and take advantage of opportunities. This can be seen in both animals and humans. However, unlike animals, human emotions often clash with socially and culturally acquired conventions and rules. In this case, these automated responses may actually be disruptive and less adaptive than consciously deliberated responses. Tears of sadness may have garnered sympathy, but it can also denote weakness and a moment where someone's defenses are down.

Emotion is beneficial because it causes an organism to carry out certain preset behaviors that have been adapted over time to lead to the best outcome. In most cases of emotion, our movements lead to developing an intense focus on the object that triggered the emotion, something that focuses all our attention. This can be seen in behaviors like freezing in place, fleeing from a threat, or nurturing our young. All these actions are caused directly because of our reactions to specific emotions. If it's not positive focus, it's negative, paranoid fixation. They both assist survival.

An example of this is when a herd of deer are grazing, and even if only one of them hears the slightest noise, the entire herd looks up and concentrates very specifically on its surroundings and is able to identify and focus on a nearby lion before fleeing. A human example might be when a parent hears their child scream from across a room. They are immediately focused on nothing but their child and develop tunnel vision until they find out what's wrong. This happens because we are inclined to have a much greater focus on the object that causes whatever emotion we are feeling.

Along with pure survival instinct, emotions also serve to alert us to threats based on our past experiences. We all develop "emotional programs" that we adopt in situations that warrant emotion. For example, we have had to learn how and whom we can trust, how to cope with failure, and how to react to death. These all come with behaviors that we have had to learn over time so that we know how to act in certain emotional situations.

Humans are a social species. The survival and success of our social lives are often based on emotion, especially the automatic and involuntary expression of them. In every social situation, we have a whole array of emotional signals that we use to lead to our end goal. If we want a conversation to last longer, we make an effort to ask more and look engaged and interested, or do the reverse if we want to leave a social setting. Evolutionary psychologists believe that we have developed a set number of emotional reactions for social situations easily interpreted by others so conclusions can be reached nonverbally.

Based on the above, the purpose of emotions is to first detect evolutionary survival cues, and then trigger reactions that have worked in the past and that we have deemed as good solutions to those problems. It is a continuous commentary on how we, and others around us, see the meaning of things. We can utilize this knowledge by paying better attention to what our emotions are telling us.

Some emotions are automatically signaled because we have such an immediate and quick reaction to them. Other emotions, such as jealousy or guilt, can be harder to identify and consciously react to. In either case, emotions help us because we are able to see what they are pointing an arrow at.

The Negativity Bias

Because emotion has the purpose of keeping us alive, there is also negativity bias, which affects how we feel. This can basically be explained as our tendency to focus a lot more on the negative things than on the positive things because they are amplified in our brain and seem to require more attention (Fiske, 1980).

There is a reason for this. Negative emotions are more noticeable to us because attending to negative events is often more important to our survival than dealing with positive events. The worst outcome when you delay a reaction to a positive event—for example, a birthday, a promotion, or a wedding—is that you celebrate a little later than you normally would have. However, with a negative event, there are much worse things that can happen if our reactions are delayed. It seems quite appropriate that we focus on dealing with negative things first, as they have the power to kill us, whereas positive events merely enhance our well-being.

There is a greater variety of options to respond and cope with potential harm than potential good. We don't even need to "cope" with good fortune—we just enjoy it.

The way we tend to fixate on negativity and worst-case scenarios is not just a temperament; it's how we have evolved to survive. There are an infinite number of ways that situations can take a turn for the worse rather than taking a turn for the better. The night before a big event, we are most often thinking about every single thing that could go wrong, not everything that could go right. If any of these possibilities actually occurs, you need to deal with them, so it's better that you imagine them and aren't caught off guard. Appropriately, negative emotions take up more mental bandwidth. Avoiding death is simply more important than eating cake.

At a basic psychological level, learning studies have also shown negativity to be an incredibly powerful motivator. Research conducted on both humans and animals showed that the desire to avoid negative reinforcement produced far stronger results than using positive reinforcement (Baumeister, 2001).

Overall, emotions are at the center of almost all that we do. Our actions and behaviors can be directly linked to the emotions that we feel. The reason for this is none other than survival. Emotions are of utmost importance so that they help us respond to situations and provoke instinctual reactions that may be the difference between survival or success, and failure. We have a strong negativity bias because we evolved to focus on that which can harm us and find a way to deal with it. Without emotion, we would not have the same response to the world or the people that surround us.

Chapter 2. Emotional Triggers

We've all heard of it and we've all felt it: a small provocation that can send our emotions spiraling in a direction that we didn't anticipate and that objectively shouldn't have any impact whatsoever.

This could be that one song that reminds you of something extremely traumatic, or maybe that one person you don't see often enough, but when you do, your emotions are out of your control. It could even be mentioning a single word, such as a name or the word "fat," that is the tip of the iceberg in terms of what it represents to you.

These are *emotional triggers*: things that elicit an immediate emotional response. There are positive ones and negative ones, but we don't need help with positive ones. Some can lead to positive emotions, like discovering an item from your childhood that you immediately associate with happiness or love. It boils down to something you have special sensitivity to, and it can impact you for the entire day or even week. With only a few words, you are feeling entirely off center and fall into a pit of anxiety, depression, guilt, or shame.

Why Do We Have Emotional Triggers?

Why are we so deeply affected by something that we rationally know should not affect us as badly as it does? Can't we be logical creatures that aren't ruled by our emotions?

Yes and no. In short, we have emotional triggers because we have lived, struggled, and come of age. No matter how lucky you have been in life, you have had moments of hardship and trauma you never want to experience again. Things that happen in the past, especially when we were children, are often ingrained deep into our minds. We may not have been able to deal with the pain or suffering or embarrassment that we felt when we were younger, so we suppress it. And years later, when we are adults, reminders of our pain can bring those feelings screaming back. It's not productive to go completely down the Sigmund Freud route and assume that all of your adult pains are the result of childhood traumas, but without a doubt, that is where the roots of many lie.

There is usually a story behind it; sometimes it isn't something you can pinpoint but a variety of events that lead to a painful idea. There is nothing wrong with you if a painful memory triggers pain; it just means you're human. It doesn't mean you're weak or mentally ill because everyone does the same. It's just a feeling that we have because of what something may lead you to think, or what something may represent to you. For instance, the pain of being constantly berated and ridiculed for being overweight as a child is something you can easily imagine to cause multiple emotional triggers in adulthood. You may be extremely sensitive about your weight, or you might have developed eating disorders to cope with those feelings of inadequacy.

How do you act when you suddenly experience great pain? You retreat into whatever habits or defense mechanisms you've developed over the years. For some, this will be physically withdrawing, while for others, it means a complete mental shutdown into a near catatonic state.

The word trigger is an important point here. The idea of an emotional *trigger* is that it is something that occurs automatically. One of the goals of this book is to move away from this automatic, involuntary path and onto a more conscious path. By learning how to identify your emotional triggers, you can start to seize control of your compulsions and respond rather than react. Once you start becoming aware of these triggers, you can begin to monitor them and realize that you can intervene in the period of time between the trigger and your response. This intervention is the key to changing the outcome of the situation and trying to get a more desirable result.

Emotional triggers often lie behind some of our worst behaviors. If you think about negative behaviors that seem automatic or out of your control, then you may just be unaware of the emotional trigger that caused it. Triggers are very personal. Different things trigger different people, and so a trigger for you may not affect another person at all.

The emotional intensity that is felt by a trigger is of a similar intensity as the initial trauma itself, which perfectly explains why anyone would want to avoid it. These triggers can be activated by any of the five senses: sight, sound, smell, touch, and taste.

When looking to better respond to your triggers, you need to identify the trigger itself first. The external stimuli may appear to be innocent, but it could be a trigger simply because of what it represents to you. It may have nothing to do with the words that someone said to you and more to do with the links you make in your mind.

Perhaps a comment is made about you never attending college. This is a fact but it may also make you think about other things you never had the chance to do or things that you missed out on. As it is a trigger, you may very well follow this train of negativity and include everything in your life that you wished you had done, and all the regrets you have over them. Maybe it will grow to include never going on that holiday you'd dreamed of or rejecting a job offer that you wish you hadn't. The following thoughts may have nothing to do with the initial trigger but your thoughts have led you there regardless.

As such, it is the *story* of the trigger that is important, no matter how significant. Finding the story behind the trigger is key to solving it and changing your responses.

Internal and External Triggers

Triggers can be external or internal. Often, they are both: there is an external event that gives rise to an internal reaction. External triggers are the event or situation that causes your reaction. They might be benign or harmful by themselves, but remember, they aren't necessarily why you might experience an emotional outbreak. Examples of external triggers include:

- Being rejected or abandoned
- Helplessness in painful situations
- Being ignored
- Being misunderstood
- When someone is angry at you
- Being mocked

- Being treated unequally
- When someone doesn't make time for you
- Being vulnerable or exposed
- When someone shows disapproval
- Being blamed or shamed
- Being judged
- When someone isn't happy to see you
- When someone is trying to control you

None of these are rare in everyday life. Yet for some, they can cause large reactions because of the internal triggers they represent. This is why people's emotions may escalate very quickly in response to a trigger, because of the deep emotions that they relate to them. In other words, the former list is a direct reminder of shortcomings in the following list:

- Acceptance
- Respect
- Being understood
- Being in control
- Attention
- Being needed or liked
- Being treated fairly
- Being included
- Predictability
- Safety
- Insecurity
- Pride
- Lack of confidence
- Love

There are certainly repeated themes. Once triggered, the response that usually occurs is to either deal with it or cope and avoid. I'll let you guess which approach feels easier and is taken 99% of the time. This tends to lead to self-destructive behavior, and also means the next time you face the same emotional trigger, it may even have a worse effect on you.

The coping mechanisms that we develop as a result can vary. We may create interpersonal conflict, act in a passive or aggressive manner, or stop communicating at all. The problem with these negative coping mechanisms is that over time they will become patterns that produce further emotional stress, drain our energy, and influence our lives and our work. You'll begin with distress about your trigger; then the distress will compound as you notice the effects of your negative coping mechanisms and how much you want to stop your behavior patterns.

These self-destructive habits may include:

- Lashing out at people
- Becoming needy and attention-seeking
- Becoming a people-pleaser and ignoring your own needs
- Completely withdrawing from others
- Deflecting blame onto others

- Becoming addicted to soothing behavior, such as food, alcohol, sex, drugs, shopping, and so on

The whole situation, from trigger to coping mechanism, is doomed from the start because of all the negativity that surrounds it.

Imagine you are at work and are asked to do a certain task, such as handing in a report or something similar that your employer expects and trusts you to complete. You do as you're told but his feedback is not ideal. Though you may have put a lot of time into the project, he is unsatisfied and finishes off by saying he is disappointed.

Those words could be the trigger for you: the idea of disappointment. It isn't so much that you have to fix the report—that's something that will only take an hour or two. It's the fact that you let someone down. Maybe you can relate that to your own childhood and a situation where your parents depended on you but, in the end, weren't able to rely on you after all. The weight of a parent's disapproval is something that is hard to accept, even as an adult, but especially as a child. Logically, you know you aren't a child any longer and the situation is different, but triggers aren't rational. Someone that is in a semi-paternal role to you, your supervisor, has given you a negative evaluation, and that brings feelings of inadequacy flooding back.

From there you become withdrawn and turn away from everyone else, especially those who care about you. Being alone only allows the negativity to fester and build further. Negative thoughts sustain themselves by adding more negativity to the fire, and you will start to berate yourself even if you're not sure why you feel so badly. Subconsciously, the story you've told yourself from childhood is in full effect. Feelings of insecurity, anger, remorse, or guilt will make themselves felt as well. You are feeding into a constant cycle where every rejection or disappointment will lead you to replicate this behavior, and this compounds as you feel badly about the behavior itself.

Does this sound familiar? You can easily recognize this as self-destructive behavior, but it's not so easy to stop the freight train when you're in the heat of the moment. This is a classic example of an external trigger (the disappointing comment from your supervisor) that digs deep into your psyche and conjures up something that is only tangentially related (the disappointment from your childhood). This isn't a sequence you can stop without deeper self-understanding.

Emotional *Needs*

Often emotional triggers are based around a certain *emotional need*—that is, the feeling that something is lacking.

For example, a common emotional need is the need to be in control, which may have stemmed from not having control at an earlier stage of your life. These needs aren't bad; in fact, they have served you extremely well in the past. The reason you have them is because at some point in your life they allowed you to reach a certain goal or enabled a certain outcome. For example, your life experiences may have taught you that success depends on maintaining control, creating a safe environment, and surrounding yourself with people that appreciate your organization.

Of course, the list of internal emotional triggers has a complete overlap with emotional needs:

- Acceptance
- Respect
- Being understood
- Being in control
- Attention
- Being needed or liked
- Being treated fairly
- Being included
- Predictability
- Safety
- Insecurity
- Pride
- Lack of confidence
- Love

However, the more you become attached to these needs, the more your mind will actively search for situations or events that threaten your needs. These needs then become emotional triggers. Someone may try to loosen your control on a situation and you may react negatively because you see them as trying to cause havoc in your life.

At this point, you need to really judge the truth of the situation. Are you really losing the need that you have? Is something actually being threatened, or is your reaction borne solely out of vicious defense?

You know the vast majority of the time, it is your emotional need that becomes the issue. You need to consciously acknowledge the need that is triggering your response or you will be enslaved to that need. If someone wants to try a new approach to an activity and asks you first, are you really giving up your control? Are you hanging on to a certain feeling rather than responding to the situation at hand? And for that matter, is the need for control as imperative to you as it once was?

Understanding emotional triggers will have very real impact on your life. You may not even realize that some of your negative habits are a result of emotional triggers. If you find that you are following distinct patterns of emotional triggers and then a reactive negative event, then it is time to do something about it. Own your emotional needs and understand that you are acting out of pain and longing—everything that occurs afterward is just a projection of this.

You cannot live in fear of something or avoid a specific circumstance for the rest of your life. Don't walk through life feeling like it is a minefield just waiting for the wrong step. There's no reason dealing with reminders of your past should be so painful and destructive.

Chapter 3. The Emotional Immune System

Emotional triggers were covered in the previous chapter, but you may have noticed the universal theme of low self-esteem that was present throughout the triggers. Many other triggers are related to this on some level because it is what makes you feel affected by a lack of approval, love, or attention, for instance.

Beyond that, self-esteem and self-worth are big factors in who we are. How we think of ourselves and the way we present ourselves to the world have a big impact on how others view us and how we approach life.

Low Self-Esteem

Let's start with what low self-esteem is. This is the feeling that you aren't good enough, that you are inadequate, that you'll be judged by others, and that others will reject you for being who you are. Many of our emotional needs and insecurities stem from this point—that you are somehow "less" than others. This creates an inevitable dynamic where you are always seeking to be accepted and seen as "equal" to others. Clearly, reinforcing your self-esteem is a foundational part of emotional resilience.

When we have higher self-esteem, we are stronger emotionally and are more resilient to stresses from our environment. We do not have the same feelings of inadequacy, and this is reflected in every aspect of our lives. This is also reflected in the title of this chapter—there's a reason people call self-esteem your emotional immune system.

When it's high, it makes you stronger and more emotionally resilient because you aren't reacting from pain; when it's low, you operate in the opposite manner.

An example of this is a study by Keiichi Onoda of Shimane University in Japan. His study found that when our self-esteem is low, we experience rejection as more viscerally painful than when our self-esteem is high. Because of this, we withdraw from others and our confidence is diminished. Having good self-esteem not only gives you feelings of higher self-confidence, but also means that you will better be able to cope with certain pressures—your internal monologue turns from "I can't do it" to "I can handle this."

Low self-esteem also makes us more vulnerable to failure. We experience greater drops in motivation and have less perseverance after suffering setbacks or failures than those with higher self-esteem. It can also make us more vulnerable to anxiety and stress. Worse still are the results from a study conducted by Lupis, Sabik, and Wolf from Brandeis University. They found those who have lower self-esteem release a higher amount of cortisol, the stress hormone, into their bloodstream when they experience stress, and it stays there for longer period of time. Low self-esteem quite literally makes you less emotionally stable. It truly functions like our real biological immune systems.

Another study led by Jeff Greenberg of the University of Arizona examined how people dealt with the anticipation of receiving a mild electrical shock. Half of the participants received an intervention that was aimed to improve their self-esteem, while the other half did not. Though they believed they were going to get shocked, no electrical shock was actually administered; it was only the expectation of it that was important. The results were clear: those whose self-esteem was boosted showed significantly less anxiety that the others.

These findings all indicate that our self-esteem is responsible for not only our attitude and behaviors, but also the physiology of our bodies as well. Higher self-esteem means that common psychological problems such as rejection, failure, anxiety, and stress are easier to cope with. Therefore, boosting our self-esteem will have an immediate effect on our emotional resilience.

For better or worse, our self-esteem also tends to have a baseline.

This is a general set level to which it commonly returns and is where people's resilience is based. The higher your baseline is, the higher your emotional resilience is. However, though there is a baseline, self-esteem is unstable enough that it fluctuates daily, if not hourly. To make things more complicated, our self-esteem is made up of not only how we feel about ourselves generally, but also how we feel about ourselves in specific areas of our lives. For example, as a parent, student, musician, or friend.

The more meaningful one of these areas is to us, the greater its impact on our overall self-esteem. If you were a professional chef and someone doesn't like the taste of your cooking, this will affect your overall self-esteem much more than for someone that doesn't think cooking is a major aspect of their identity. Similarly, if you pride yourself on being a good parent and trying to do the best for your children, criticisms toward your parenting skills will affect you much more than other criticisms you may receive.

The extent that something will affect you is all about how core an area is to your overall identity. Knowing this means that you can understand why you are being affected by something and means you can better control your reaction and your self-esteem in response. Instead of feeling your self-worth plummet because someone doesn't like your meal, you can identify that it is important to you and instead ask them how to improve. Identifying the problem means that you have something to fix, instead of just generalizing and thinking that you will never be able to succeed because of one criticism.

Improving Your Self-Esteem

It's clear that boosting our self-esteem can improve our emotional immune system. But how do we do this when our self-esteem is low? Isn't that like telling a slow runner to simply run faster if they want to improve their running?

One of the keys is to pursue activities that remind you of your self-worth. Identify something you're good at; perhaps it's cooking or maybe it is a particular sport. Once you have that activity in mind, make sure you allocate time to actually engage in these activities. Self-esteem is built up when you achieve and improve in areas of your life that matter. If you pride yourself on being a good cook, throw more dinner parties and try to perfect difficult recipes. If you pride yourself on being a good runner, try for a new personal best, sign up for races or marathons, and train for them. Identify your core strengths (everyone has them, even you) and find opportunities and careers that allow you to capitalize on them.

By focusing on your strengths and successes, self-esteem that was once restricted to certain domains will begin to transfer to the rest of your life. This will allow you to work on your weaknesses in privacy and safety because you will be firm in the knowledge that it is your strengths that define you, not your weaknesses. When you feel good about what you can do, not what you can't, you can concentrate and remember these strengths in times of hardship.

Self-criticism is something that is hard to ignore. We all want to be better and can't help but judge much of what we do too harshly, even if we wouldn't judge another for it. Even if it feels compelling or motivating, self-criticism is almost entirely useless. This is because you're focusing on the negative things instead of the positive. If your goal is to enhance your self-esteem, you need to substitute self-criticism with self-compassion.

To do this, any time your self-critical inner monologue kicks in, take a moment to consider the criticisms themselves. Imagine if a close friend was in the same situation. Would you have the same reaction? We tend to be far more compassionate to our friends than to ourselves. Think about what you would say to a friend in your situation and direct those comments at yourself instead. Doing so will avoid damaging your self-esteem further with critical thoughts. Instead, you will be able to build up your self-esteem and treat yourself less harshly as a result.

For example, imagine yourself trying to engage in a new hobby. Learning a new skill is always difficult, and you know this. However, you find yourself not showing even the slightest bit of improvement or success. Self-critical thoughts may begin at this point. It may not even be because you aren't very good at one particular activity. Often it may spiral into thoughts of every other thing that you may or may not be good at.

This is where you need to stop and take a step back. What would you say to a friend that was also struggling with one of their new activities? Chances are you'd probably say something much more positive, something about keeping motivation and practicing again and again until you succeed. You may feel this like this is sugarcoating the issue a bit, but it's also the truth and not the worst possible interpretation of the events at hand. Now direct that positivity at yourself and replace those negative self-critical thoughts you had before. You're only human and you're allowed to not be perfect. By giving yourself a chance to fail and by being okay with that failure, you're really giving yourself a chance to succeed and thus boosting your self-esteem.

The Perfection Myth

Myths of perfection are a big part of our unrealistic and too-harsh expectations of ourselves. Rationally, we know that nobody is perfect, but we still hold ourselves up to ideals that we may never be able to reach. Buying into these myths of what is and isn't acceptable will only hurt you and the other people in your life. You are just setting yourself up for disappointment for that inevitable moment when you realize you won't reach perfection.

Life isn't like a movie or song. Simply reminding yourself of this is a good reality check when you're daydreaming of perfection. Reality will almost always clash with ideals of perfection, and this may lead to a dissatisfaction that can never be fixed. It can harm or even possibly lead to the end of relationships, jobs, projects, and other important things in your life.

Perfection is simply unattainable for any of us. This is something we need to accept. You're never going to be absolutely perfect. You're never going to have the perfect body, the perfect life, the perfect relationship, the perfect children, or the perfect home. Even if you think you have a degree of perfection, there will always be someone with more of something, or who is better at something.

Perfection is just an artificial ideal created by society and perpetuated by popular media.

We seek it because it is impossible to escape, but once we understand that it doesn't exist, we will be better off because of it.

Take hold of your accomplishments as you achieve them. Acknowledge them for their actual value. Stop devaluing your achievements by saying you could have done better or it wasn't entirely perfect, or even that it wasn't a big deal for you. Appreciate them for what they are: achievements in their own right.

It may help to keep a journal or a list of things that you accomplish each day as a reminder of all you can achieve. Everything from large triumphs to tiny victories. Not only will it lift your spirits when you have feelings of self-doubt, but it will inspire you to do more, just so you can write more. You may choose to write daily, or maybe even once a week or month. It doesn't matter how you choose to take note of your accomplishments, just that you do. Because small goals are easy and quick to accomplish, you will build momentum each time you achieve something and then strive to keep going.

When something doesn't go perfectly, it's not a reflection of you. A key part of self-esteem is learning to differentiate between circumstances and your identity. Your circumstances are external events you may not have control over. You are not your mistakes. Your identity is not based on the last thing that you did or did not do successfully. It is more useful and effective to concentrate on things that you can change as opposed to things that you can't.

For example, perhaps you have decided you want to be more fit and healthy. You start eating healthy foods and exercising several times a week. You have changed your entire life around, banned all sugar from the house, and only allowed healthy things. The problem is that one day you get a terrible craving and eat decadent chocolate cake instead of the healthy meal you were planning.

Before thoughts of failure kick in, or the feelings of inadequacy because you didn't successfully stick to your plan, take a moment to put things into perspective. Making one bad eating decision is not fundamental to who you are as a person. It should only be treated as a mistake that you will try to rectify, not as a sin that will forever mean that you weren't good enough. Remember the rest of your victories over the week or month. Instead of focusing on one decision that doesn't define who you are, focus on the decision itself. Perhaps you might rework your diet so that on occasion you may have food you love in smaller quantities that won't affect your overall health.

The key here is to focus on how to improve, not on what you think you've done wrong by not reaching perfection. Your self-esteem will improve if you focus less on your perceived failures and more on trying to strive for success.

Being Realistic

A final important factor, especially in the above example, is the need to be realistic and set correct expectations.

Self-esteem is useless if it is based upon a version of you that does not exist or no longer exists. Claiming that you were a certain weight in high school, or that you could run so many miles when you were younger, or that you were once able to solve a particular calculus equation at one point in time isn't something that you need to dwell on. That's simply not who you are anymore, so always comparing yourself to that person is an exercise in futility.

You are different, and that's not necessarily negative. We all have skills that we pick up and lose as life goes on. Just because you used to be much better at something, or able to do it at all, doesn't mean you need to make comparisons to your past self. You may have lost some skills but perhaps you've also gained some in the process. Today you may be a better cook than you ever were, a better writer, or be more business-savvy than ever before.

For every skill or aspect you liked about your former self, another has taken its place that is equally praise-worthy. Don't sit around and reminisce about how you could once play the guitar really well. Value yourself on things that you are able to do right now. If it really means that much to you, you can very easily pick up the instrument and learn how to play again—most of us will never take this step, so it's clearly not that important to us, and is used primarily to beat ourselves up via comparisons.

Evaluate yourself based upon who you are at this very moment, not some past version of yourself and not some future version that you believe you should be. Your self-image should change and adjust constantly to match who you are and who you've become, based on current abilities and skills. Adjust your beliefs about yourself so that they are realistic and focus on your current strengths, goals, and aspirations.

In this way, you will be accepting yourself for who you are, and your self-esteem will lift as a result. We are always told when we are younger to stop comparing ourselves to others because we are all different and all have different paths, goals, and decisions in life. By the same principle, we should stop comparing ourselves to who we used to be or who we think we should be. By accepting who we are right now, we will be infinitely more satisfied in all aspects of our lives.

Chapter 4. Defining the Emotional Spectrum

We've discussed the purpose of emotions and their importance in life, but there is more to understanding and interpreting your emotional needs.

First, to be clear, this isn't a book about suppressing emotions. In fact, it's the opposite. Understanding and feeling your emotions is paramount in dealing with unexpected hardships. However, one of the foundational levels of understanding, being *accurate* with your emotions, is a piece of the puzzle for emotional resilience.

In doing so, we must define the entire emotional spectrum so you know what you are dealing with and can react in the most optimal way. A doctor is only effective if she can diagnose the underlying sickness. Once that is achieved, she can prescribe medicine and actions to help that particular sickness. We can't seek to strengthen our emotional resolve if we are taking a stab in the dark at what we're feeling. We might know what our needs are, but those can manifest in very different ways for all of us.

Emotional Suppression

Most people are unaware of how crucial it is to pay attention and listen to your emotions instead of trying to ignore or suppress them. People are often under the false impression that if you ignore a certain feeling, it will just go away, or if you ignore your emotional needs, then you won't have them anymore.

That's not emotional resilience; that's stifling yourself.

There is no shame in feeling your emotions. Suppressing emotions will only lead to you feelings festering, and you may lash out at a later time. This is the reason that therapy is so important to some, because keeping in emotions is unhealthy, but talking them out, especially with a neutral third party, makes you feel much better.

Emotional suppression isn't always pointless, and there's a reason we feel compelled to do it sometimes. Often it even serves an essential purpose. Sufferers of a severe traumatic injury will find that their body may automatically fall into a state of physiological shock. This blocks all feeling and sensation, numbing consciousness to protect the mind from whatever traumatic event has occurred. Shock quite literally keeps people alive and allows them to act in self-preservation. Similarly, people that have experienced physical, emotional, or sexual abuse commonly report feeling numb, losing consciousness, or having an out-of-body experience where they seem to be observing the scene from above. In cases such as these, emotional suppression serves a purpose in protecting the mind and is a necessary first step in the healing process.

It isn't always during harsh traumatic events that emotional suppression may be of use. We all learn from a young age that acting out by letting our emotions control us will not get us what we desire. A child knows that no matter how much a parent, teacher, or other authority figure may anger them, it rarely helps to express their rage. Often, it will make matters much worse. Though you may be entirely grief-stricken, there is a time and place for your tears. Crying does not always help, especially around some who do not abide by tears or when the time and energy that it takes to cry will interfere with something else that needs attention.

The same applies to fear. Expressing fear to others can undermine your ability to lead, interfere with the immediate need for action, or mean that others will see you as unreliable.

There is a certain code that is put in place in every social group that you belong to. There are certain things that you would say to your friends that you might not say to your family, and vice versa. All social groups develop their own set rules, which govern the acceptable and unacceptable times for emotional expression.

Many times, you will find yourself in a social setting where one or more people are expressing emotion and you find that you must suppress your own so that there will not be total chaos. If all members of a group let go of their emotional barriers, havoc will ensue. In our society, forming polite, civil, working social groups means that individuals need to learn to control their emotional energy.

This means understanding when it is appropriate and acceptable to release your emotion or build up those of others, and when it is appropriate to rein in your feelings and tame your emotions. Maturing socially is usually a matter of learning to rein in our natural but childish tendency for emotion expression.

The problem arises when we never get around to expressing anger, fear, sadness, or anxiety. We never experience a catharsis or let ourselves feel, and eventually it becomes a habit that is hard to break out of. It becomes your automatic reaction. There may be circumstances when you must suppress your emotions for a brief while to tend to something else, but keep in mind that this must be brief. You need to find a way to release your emotions instead of suppressing them.

In a 2012 study, psychotherapist Eric L. Garland of Florida State University gathered 58 adults in treatment for alcohol dependence and measured their responses to stress based on heart rate when exposing them to alcohol-related cues. The results found that those who restrained their thinking and suppressed their emotions more had much stronger stress responses to the cues than those who suppressed less frequently.

Even if you think you have successfully bypassed a topic, there is no guarantee that your subconscious has also stopped dwelling on it. In 2011, psychologist Richard A. Bryant of the University of New South Wales in Sydney conducted a study where half the participants were told to suppress an unwanted thought prior to sleep. Those who tried to suppress their thoughts reported that they dreamed about it more, a phenomenon called dream rebound.

Both of these studies indicate that emotional suppression not only doesn't work, but can also be immensely harmful. It can cause you to fixate more on what you are avoiding, and can be detrimental to your physical health. As if this wasn't evidence enough, another study in the United States by experts at the Harvard School of Public Health and the University of Rochester showed that those who fail to say or express how they feel increased their risk of premature death from all causes by about 35%. When researchers evaluated specific causes of death, they uncovered that the risks increased by 47% for heart disease and 70% for cancer.

Death rates are highest among those most likely to bottle up their emotion rather than express it to others and let them know how they feel. With the consequences so high, it seems even more foolish to avoid expressing your emotions. In fact, doing so will mean that they will come out in unpredictable and damaging ways.

Some emotions occur so regularly that we cannot consciously suppress them. Instead, we become numb to them. They are always there, under the surface, but we simply ignore their presence so much that we forget we are even feeling them. This is called emotional numbness. Consider it similar to when you wear a piece of clothing that you thought was uncomfortable at first but eventually get used to it. Or when you enter a room and immediately smell something but after a few minutes it doesn't bother you as much anymore. Even though you're numb to these emotions and are no longer aware of them, it doesn't mean they are gone forever. They lurk under the surface and will resurface at a later time, most likely adding to the intensity of your negative emotions and fueling your emotional outburst.

Emotional Granularity

Since it is clear that emotional suppression is not the answer, what should you do instead? *Emotional granularity* is the answer. This is the process of understanding what you are feeling by putting a specific name on it. It seems insignificant, but you will be able to release some of the intensity of the emotion just by allowing it to make itself known. There's a certain amount of tension from a lack of clarity about your feelings.

People that have finely tuned feelings and are very in touch with their emotions are said to exhibit emotional granularity. It's not about being able to complicatedly label every emotion you have or just expand your vocabulary so that you can do this. It is about experiencing the world, and thus yourself, more precisely. By doing this, you will be able to better identify what it is exactly that you're feeling, and by identifying it, you will be able to understand the reasoning behind it.

Emotional granularity was coined in the 1990s by Lisa Feldman Barrett, who asked hundreds of volunteers to track and monitor their emotional experiences for weeks or months. All the participants in the study used the same vocabulary to define their emotions with standard words such as "sad," "angry," and "afraid." However, the study found that some people used the words to refer to distinct and differing experiences. Each word represented multiple emotional concepts and feelings. Others in the study lumped these words together under a single conceptual meaning, basically alluding to the feelings of being miserable.

According to Barrett, the greater the granularity, the "more precisely" you can experience yourself and your world. This means that you can pinpoint how you feel and better identify a solution. By using different words for different emotions and individualizing your vocabulary, there are many more benefits to your emotional health. We become what we label ourselves, and this can either help or hurt you.

People who were able to learn diverse emotional concepts were able to understand more finely tailored emotions. Emotional granularity can have a large influence on your health and well-being because it equips your brain to handle a wider range of emotions that you may experience. In other words, by knowing what you're feeling, you know better what the causes and underlying emotional needs are, and you know how to solve it.

For example, you may be feeling a combination of sadness, boredom, restlessness, and yearning, and without the proper understanding of your emotions, you may just generalize it as feeling sad.

But this does not solve the problem because it may not be exactly what you're feeling. However, this all changes if you have emotional granularity and are able to correctly identify your emotion as loneliness. Lumping emotions together means that you may not know how to deal with them, but identifying them all as distinct, independent emotions promotes understanding. Acting to fix a general feeling of sadness is a far different course of action than acting to fix loneliness.

The better your understanding of what it is exactly that you're experiencing, the more flexibility your brain has in anticipating or prescribing actions. It is easy to generalize or dismiss what you are feeling, but it is much more effective to give it some thought and pinpoint exactly what your emotional state is.

One step to take in increasing your emotional vocabulary is to take a look at the true spectrum of emotions. Quick, try to name as many emotions are you can. How many did you come up with? Here, the spectrum is represented by Robert Plutchik's wheel of emotions (courtesy of wired.com):

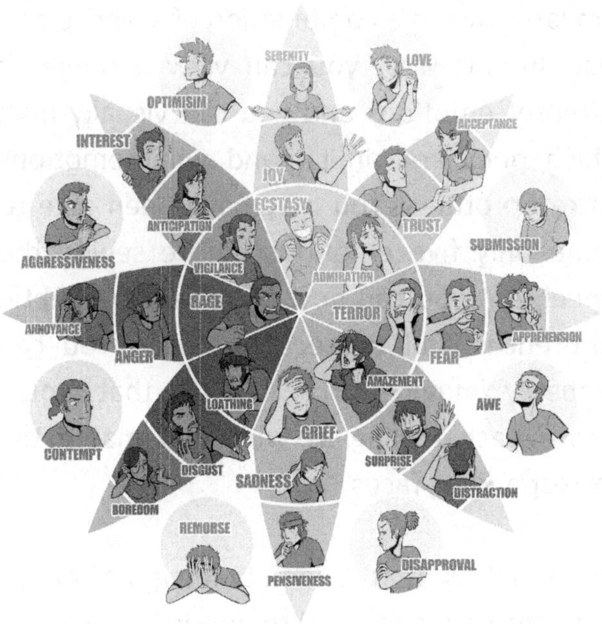

Emotional Diversity

The purpose of this wheel is to provide a visual method for identifying a variety of emotions and to help relate them all to each other. Emotions on the outside, such as love, are a combination of two emotions in the petals beside them, in this case joy and trust. Similarly, awe is a combination of surprise and fear. In this way, you can view a range of different emotions and you can visually map which ones are similar and what emotions make up others. You may have been able to name only five emotions before seeing the wheel, but you can now see there are subtle differences and degrees for each. You can probably imagine circumstances that would create each feeling as well, and match the corresponding faces.

The point is that understanding emotional diversity is fundamental to our well-being.

A study led by Anthony Ong of Cornell University investigated the effect of emotion on health. The study suggested that happiness is too often considered as the emotion most strongly connected to a healthier body. The researchers found that feeling a wide range of emotions—what they termed emotional diversity, or *emodiversity*—may be the link to better health. This includes negative emotions and is another powerful argument for understanding emotional granularity and familiarizing yourself with Plutchik's wheel.

Ong had participants keep a journal of their emotions for 30 days. The participants had to rate the extent to which they experienced 16 positive emotions that day. Happiness, enthusiasm, determination, pride, inspiration, and strength were among the positive emotions. They also recorded any negative emotions they experienced, such as sadness, anger, shame, and guilt. Emodiversity was measured by the number of different emotions felt by a person, the overall distribution, and the number of times each emotion was felt.

Ong found that people who experienced a wider range of emotions, including negative ones, were better at regulating emotions, keeping their cool, and refraining from using alcohol as a coping mechanism. He explained by comparing the emotions to a natural ecosystem, which is healthier when each various species serves its specific, functional role. If any one species becomes too dominant, it destroys the balance of the entire ecosystem and causes, for example, the dodo bird to go extinct.

Emodiversity similarly helps us prioritize and regulate our behavior so that we can cope and adapt with any given situation. By experiencing many different but specific emotions, there is more adaptive value than experiencing fewer emotions or more general ones. This is because the more specific emotions provide richer and more useful information to guide our decisions and how we face challenges.

For example, if you identify that you are feeling a variety of emotions such as anger, shame, and sadness, this will be more useful to you than just saying you feel "bad," which is a general term that doesn't provide you with much insight on how to solve the problem.

By specifying anger, you can then delve into what or who made you angry. By specifying shame, you are implying that you yourself have done something that you may regret. By specifying sadness, you may believe that the cause of your current emotional state shouldn't have happened and you want to fix the issue. All these points of action simply come from being able to identify your real emotions. If you had just stopped at feeling "bad," you may not have done anything at all. Indulging in the full range of negative emotions simply prepares you.

Admitting you have emotional needs is only the first step to emotional resilience. This chapter takes the additional steps of understanding emotional granularity and the overall importance attaching a name to feelings. Indulge in your emotions and feel the entire spectrum of possibilities. Suppressing emotions is something we engage in for self-protection, but counterintuitively, it will only weaken our emotional well-being. Don't be afraid to feel all you can and feel deeply.

Chapter 5. Recognition, Regulation, and Response

Our emotions are not always reliable. They are geared toward ensuring our species survives, but that isn't usually our goal these days.

We now know that suppressing them is not the answer and that you should allow yourself to feel even your darkest of feelings so that you can release them. But there is a time and a place for indulging in all of the emotional needs we have discussed, and sometimes you may just not be in the right situation to do so. Regulating your emotions means dealing with your emotional needs in a healthy and socially acceptable way. This chapter will explain how you can release your emotions in healthy and non-damaging ways that won't make you a depressed outcast or embark on a downward spiral.

Emotions are a constant part of our lives. Every minute of every day we will feel something, and our emotions can change in an instant. There are highs and lows that you experience every day, and how you deal with them can significantly affect your mental state and well-being. But we can't wear all of our emotions on our sleeves all the time. Our ability to regulate the vast number of emotions that you feel also affects how the people in your life perceive you.

That doesn't mean that everyone is always watching to see how you react to every situation. It simply means that inappropriate emotions will be noticed by all. Laughing at a text message during a funeral will likely mean that all those in the room will be irritated or resentful to some degree. Reacting with rage at a driver who cuts you off in traffic will also garner unfavorable attention. It can be difficult when you are caught up in these moments to regulate your emotions and think of the consequences, but the more you do it, the more it becomes habitual.

Benefits of Regulation

Emotional regulation is beneficial because it helps you control many of the self-defeating behaviors that stem from emotional spikes. These include self-sabotage, the ensuing downward spiral, comparison, and negative self talk, to name a few.

The first is self-sabotage. We can all be accused of having thoughts that will sabotage our success. This is when we don't even try because of the risk of failure, or give up on something because we don't think we will succeed. Imagine running a marathon and giving up halfway because you're in last place and to continue would feel like a waste of time. You might be in first place but self-sabotage because of your negative beliefs. Regulating your emotions means quieting the inner voice that tells you can't, and pushing on. It means you'll keep persevering even though your mental state isn't optimistic.

Next is the downward spiral. This is the endless cycle that starts with something mundane. Perhaps you have a presentation at work the following day and you feel a bit nervous. Then you start stressing about your nerves and how your nerves will ruin your presentation. Then you become nervous that your stress about your nerves will ruin your day. This continues into a downward spiral that you may never be able to leave because you are so busy concentrating on the possibilities of failure. Regulating your emotions means cutting this process off as soon as you notice it happening. Instead of spending your time stressing versus rehearsing, you'll tell yourself that nerves are perfectly normal and are actually a good sign.

Next is comparison. Comparing yourself to others is illogical for many reasons. It's the same as being in a competition where one participant sings and one dances; each are too different to compare. Perhaps you are jealous because someone in your company for only a few months has already gotten a promotion whereas you haven't. Regulating your emotions allows you to step back and realize that they may be in a completely different position than you are or that they have been working so hard that they deserve it, but that doesn't mean you are worth any less. If you constantly compare, realize that you have extremely imperfect information and that you are inevitably comparing your worst moments to someone's best hits.

Last is negative self-talk. These are the thoughts that you have about yourself that reduce you to a mythical version of yourself, except, instead of a hero, this version of you is the butt of every joke and the enemy of the story. Negative self-talk is when you blame anything negative that occurs on yourself, and anything positive that happens on good luck and fortune. You are responsible for anything bad that happens, and other people are responsible for anything good that happens. Negative self-talk is along the same lines as self-sabotage. By regulating your emotional thinking, you will understand that your internal narrative does not reflect reality.

Those are all examples where emotional regulation can help turn around your negative emotional states. It doesn't mean stopping, ignoring, or even overcoming them; it means taking perspective and keeping an even keel whenever possible. But how do you go about doing this?

The Five Steps of Regulation

Some emotional responses require no regulation—mostly positive ones. Laughing at a friend's joke or crying in a sad film are all acceptable behaviors in their specific contexts. If an emotion is appropriate and helps you feel better, then there is no need to regulate. However, for example, a common emotion to regulate is impatience and anger at waiting in a long line. It might make you feel better, but it is neither appropriate nor productive. How can you regulate something like this by either expressing this frustration in alternative means or regaining your emotional composure? If you do need to regulate your emotions, there are five steps to follow that will help you achieve this. Stanford psychologist J.J. Gross came up with a five-step methodology for regulating emotion.

The first step is to select the situation.

This means that you should avoid seek to situations that trigger unwanted emotions whenever possible. Imagine that you have recently decided to partake in a marathon. You've been training hard, eating healthily, and increasing your endurance. However, maybe you find that you lose motivation when you see others at the gym and they seem to be running so much faster than you or lifting so much more than you. This is where you can employ this step. Maybe you will go for more runs outside instead of in the gym. It doesn't mean that you are escaping from your problems. It simply means that to keep your emotions up, you chose not to surround yourself with things that might bring you negativity. Remove yourself from dangerous situations so you don't have to regulate at all. You have more of a say than you think.

The next step is to modify the situation.

This is when you cannot employ step one. Let's say that you work late and choose not to run outside because it's cold and dark. You know that at the gym you normally have feelings of inadequacy and you wish to reduce this. This is where you have to face the situation you have been trying to avoid, so you need to modify it to reduce its impact on you. You modify the situation to insulate your emotions by actively changing the terms for success. Just because you can't go as fast as someone doesn't mean you can't run for as long. If you adjust the rules and make it so you are competing only with yourself, then you are in a can't-lose situation.

The third step is to shift your focus.

When you can't avoid or modify a situation, you can always change what you focus your attention on. If you're upset by something, you fixate on it to your own detriment. Instead of being preoccupied by runners that are faster than you, instead shift your focus to the gym-goers you are much, much faster than you. You can also shift your focus to yourself and your own running—perhaps you aren't running so fast because you're always distracted and discouraged. Concentrate on improving yourself and reaching your own goals instead of beating someone else. Whatever negative thoughts seem to be taking your attention, switch to positive ones.

Step four is to change your thoughts.

At the core of our deepest emotions are the beliefs that drive them. You're sad when you lose something, angry when your goals are thwarted, and happy when you believe you have good coming your way. By knowing this, you can change your emotions by changing the beliefs that sustain them. Your negative belief is that everyone at the gym is judging you and inspecting you for your failures—therefore, your emotions will reflect that. This is where you need to change your thoughts. To do this, think about how you view others at the gym. Most of the time, you don't really care what they do, or you think their performance is better than yours. By that reasoning, what if they feel the same about you? Believe that people don't judge and aren't even paying attention to you, and your emotions will follow and relax.

The fifth and final step of emotion regulation, when all else fails, is to change your response.

This is true regulation. This is when you no other steps of this process work and you find yourself feeling without limits. Maybe you feel utterly destroyed, decide to give up, and are very close to tears or rage. Take a deep breath to gather yourself, close your eyes, and pause. Gather your inner reserve and force yourself at least to change your facial expression and *keep it in*. Obviously, you won't be able to. I did mention that emotional suppression was unhealthy, but this is different because you want to keep yourself together for social purposes. The reasoning behind this is that most emotions are instantaneous reactions, and when we reflect on them, we just might respond differently. By pausing in your tracks and taking a few moments to let them dwell on your emotions, you will find that you can actively regulate them.

Healthy Self-Talk

Self-talk is a habit that many of us may have as a way to deal with our thoughts. Maybe it's a subconscious muttering while we are preoccupied with another task, or maybe it's a conscious discussion about what you should do in a situation.

It doesn't have to be out loud; it can just be a silent communication in your mind. Self-talk is great when it is positive and reinforces constructive thoughts. Negative self-talk is usually destructive and should be avoided because of its self-defeating results. Constantly having negative thoughts and comments on your mind will reflect in your self-esteem. If you are frequently putting yourself down, then it is easy to see why your confidence or self-worth may be low as well. To get into the habit of healthy self-talk for better emotional regulation, there are a few steps that you can try out.

The first step is one of awareness. If you are in a habit of negative self-talk, it is hard to change this to positive self-talk without being acutely and realistically aware of the thoughts that run through your mind. You can't stop interrupting people if you have no idea you are doing it. If you have a long history of negative self-talk, then it may be difficult to make this switch. You may not even be aware of the times you say negative things to yourself because it may come as an automatic reaction.

Some common negative phrases may not even mean much to you, but their effect can be profound. A common phrase is saying to yourself, "I can't." This is something that you may not even notice after a while, but every time you tell yourself you can't do something, it negates the possibility of even trying. Another phrase is that "it's too difficult." For our purposes, healthier self-talk consists of avoiding phrases like "I'm so frustrated" and other negative emotions. These phrases can cause a mental block that will prevent you from being successful at a task simply because your mind has already decided that you've failed. When you say it, you live up to it for better or worse.

If you find yourself in one of these moments with one of these thoughts, then you need to stop immediately. Find a way to contradict these thoughts, whether it is in your mind or out loud. One way is that any time you think "I can't," immediately say "Yes, I can." When you think "it's too difficult," immediately say "No, it's not." If these become an automatic reaction to negative self-talk, then you will be able to mentally convince yourself of the positive thoughts instead of dwelling on the negative ones.

If you are in a situation where negative thoughts seem to bombard you and you don't know what to do, then stop again. Say to yourself, "What is my next step?" When faced with an actual question that needs an answer, you will be less preoccupied with your internal anxiety and more with how to manage the present. You cannot change the past, nor can you control the future. What you can do is take certain steps that allow you to predict the most probable future, and be more comfortable with what can happen.

For example, imagine that you are doing a last-minute work project where something has gone wrong and you're not sure if you will finish. Your thoughts may be in a state of panic and anxiety. You aren't making much progress, and all you can think about are the mistakes that led you to that point. You begin to think, "I'll never be able to finish in time. I'm such a terrible student. I don't deserve good grades." This is the point where you must stop everything immediately and take a moment to assess your situation.

The first thing you should do is take the last thought you have and say, "Yes, I can," whether it is out loud or firmly in your mind. The next thing you need to do is ask yourself, "What can I do right now?" The answer to that is almost always very obvious. In this situation, it may just be that you need to do a bit more research, collate all your documents, and send it where it needs to go. A good idea is to say the steps out loud or write them down somewhere where you can cross them off as it's done. A visual reminder of your progress is sometimes very important for your motivation.

By focusing not on what happened to get you in your situation and instead on what you can do to move forward, you will change your negative self-talk to positive courses of action. Blame and guilt are useless; steps to fix problems are far more helpful. Taking these steps requires you to focus your thoughts and inner talk on the here and now, which is the best way to dismiss negativity.

Recognize Your Narrative

We all have our own personal narratives that shape who we are. Everyone in the world is the sum total of their own personal narratives. You would not be the person you are today if you didn't have the same childhood, the same struggles, the same failures, and the same successes. When someone asks you to tell them your life story, what is it that you tell them? What do you focus on and what do you leave out? You are the one who assigns all the meaning there is to your life and experience. No one else can determine what you think or feel. This is your narrative, and it is essential to assign the right meaning and to tell yourself the most accurate and helpful story about your life.

To regulate your emotions better, you need to recognize your personal narrative and change it. If this seems easier said than done, it isn't. You are the sole person that defines your narrative, so you are the sole person who dictates how it should proceed. Changing your narrative isn't about changing your life; it's about the way you perceive it.

There are two types of narratives for our purposes: a disempowering one and an empowering one. Most of us tend to skew toward the disempowering narrative, but the empowering narrative is what gives us emotional regulation and resilience. There are four steps to this.

The first is to identify your current story. How would you describe the narrative that you're telling yourself? Think about the words you are using and the emotional impact behind them. Are they only descriptive, and if so, what are they describing? Think about the feelings generated from your story and what parts you are drawn to and what parts have more meaning.

The second is to evaluate the content of your story. Are you being empowered or disempowered? Is it a story of limiting belief? Does your story boost you up, empower you to succeed, and strive to build you up and push you forward, or does your story focus on the struggles, the failures, the disempowering moments, and the constant hardships? What are you downplaying and emphasizing from a bystander perspective? Are you ignoring your talents and fixating on the rare times you falter? The focus of the story is what defines its effect.

Third is to characterize the outcomes of your story. This requires complete honesty. What does your story do to you? You must be able to honestly say if it is helping you or only hindering your progress. Does it serve as fuel to push you forward or is it draining you of all hope and positive energy? Are you proud to tell your story or somewhat embarrassed? This step is crucial because it forces you to think about the result. The only way to do this is to be honest with yourself by looking as clearly as possible at the outcomes you're experiencing.

The fourth step is to reframe your story using new metaphors. You are not telling yourself something that isn't true to make you feel better. When you change your narrative, it is not your life that you are changing; it is the way that you view it. It is still authentic, but your thinking is shifted so that you reframe the story under a new light.

For example, when you describe a series of continuous failures, you are only able to see them as the opposite of success. All of your subsequent actions are then interpreted under the same light, under a limiting narrative. You may say that you didn't land interview after interview, you didn't succeed at a single position or role that you applied for, and that you failed consistently. However, when you shift your thinking, the outcome is different. Instead you will think, "I tried for position after position and didn't let my failures stop me. I didn't get the one role I wanted but I never let that stop me from trying to get another interview and another after that."

This is a shift in thinking, not the story itself. Both have the same content but both have a different perspective, and it is the perspective that ultimately matters.

Positive metaphors are the key to viewing your story under a different light. A metaphor for this example may be baking. There are a million ways to make a cake and a million and one ways that it may not work. When it fails, it simply means the recipe is wrong and you can change the ingredients to fix it. Alternatively, sometimes cake isn't always the answer and you find that you like pudding just as much. The fault is not with you, the baker, necessarily. The key here is to choose a metaphor that is relevant to you.

Following these four steps will help you identify your narrative and recognize whether it needs to be changed or not. Think about what stories you are telling yourself and others about you. Are your personal narratives serving you or are you serving your personal narratives? Do you have the courage and tenacity to change your story if that is what's called for?

Psychological Distance

We all know that sometimes a little distance from a situation is necessary to be able to view it properly. Sometimes you are just far too close to a situation to have any kind of objectivity. Creating psychological distance is when you view your circumstances and behavior the same as a bystander would to disassociate and gain perspective.

Finding the appropriate distance from an event may be hard to achieve if you are particularly attached or emotional about it. As mentioned, the goal in creating psychological distance is to imagine yourself looking back at an event from an outside perspective. This gives you more objectivity, which tends to be the opposite of emotional outbursts.

One method is to imagine you are in a movie theater and you are viewing the movie up on a screen. You have complete power to play with the film—rewind, fast-forward, pause, or reverse.

Imagine eating popcorn while you do it. The character in the film isn't you anymore; it is someone else playing the role. By doing this, you are disassociating yourself from the experience and watching it from a different perspective. Try to identify the flaws in your thinking upon viewing yourself on the screen. Identify the humor in the situation, reabsorb news, and try to think about it in a different way. Laugh at moments that seem exaggerated now that you look back.

This change of perspective from first person to third means that things will be less intense and not as likely to hurt you on a deep level. Observe as if you a stranger, a friend, a critic, or a relative.

For example, perhaps the event that you are looking back on is a large fight with your significant other. Things may have been said that were entirely unreasonable or exaggerated. Claims may have been made, accusations thrown, and someone may have just stormed out. By observing it objectively, you will realize that you didn't mean it when you said you hated his mother, and it was more than funny when he said he hated your cooking, because you know he doesn't. The main idea is that you develop a new perspective on the events and know what needs to be changed or solved in the future.

Remove yourself from the heat of the moment as quickly as possible, and emotions suddenly become hyperbolic and even silly in hindsight.

React versus Respond

The diagram above shows the difference between reacting and responding. Overall, emotional regulation begins and ends with this diagram.

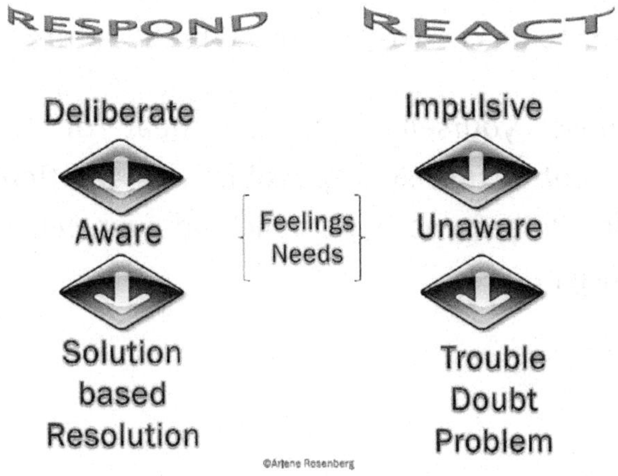

To *react* to a situation means a complete lack of regulation because there is no thought. It is impulsive, short-term thinking. To *respond* is to take time to consider the alternatives and make a decision based on the information you have. It may not always be the right one, but you won't be acting on impulse or elevated emotions.

It isn't just about controlling what you feel, but also thinking rationally about what the best course of action is. Focus less on your intense emotional impulses and more on desired outcomes and rational decisions.

Let's return to the previous example: the fight between a couple. It is important to look at the cause of the event, or the moment before you had your reaction or response. In this situation, it may have been that you wanted the two of you to spend the holidays with your family and that they wanted to spend it with theirs.

A reaction to this might mean that you immediately discount the other person's opinions and assume that they just didn't want to be with your family. You might not dwell too hard on the real reason but just begin to throw blame, feel anger, and then cause a fight that could have been avoided.

Responding would be entirely different. The first step of responding is to take a moment to think and ask why. The answer may be that they haven't seen their family in a longer time. This brief pause of consideration allows you to understand the other person's perspective and allows a rational discussion where both people will be satisfied or, at the very least, a conclusion will be reached. Regulation is almost never *easy*, but it is *simple*.

Chapter 6. The Heat of the Moment

Self-awareness and an understanding of the origin of your emotions are more important than you may think. It isn't just about why you feel a certain way, but also about how that feeling took root. It's fine to understand those emotions in hindsight, and I would hope that information is available, but it is infinitely more helpful when you can identify something in the heat of the moment and know how to act.

Sometimes we find ourselves falling into a loop where we are simply in an autopilot state of acting and thinking, which will always lead to undesirable outcomes. Your feelings get hurt, you shout and react, and you compound your negative feelings with guilt and shame.

These automated actions are very difficult to see in the heat of the moment because we are so used to doing them without thinking. This is the reason why building self-awareness and understanding the patterns of your thought and behavior are essential for emotional resiliency. Without this understanding, you will only be able to address the symptoms and not the cause. Interrupt your automatic reactions through slowing down and deciphering each part of the process.

The ABC Loop

The ABC Loop is a classic behavioral therapy technique that considers all the elements that contribute to a behavior. It stands for Antecedent, Behavior, and Consequence. The middle section, the behavior, is often called the Behavior of Interest, and the technique works by looking at the before and after to understand why the behavior in the middle occurred. It's also what you want to examine and regulate or control—hence, the increased scrutiny on it.

Let's begin with Antecedent. This is the environment, the events, or the preceding the Behavior of Interest. Anything that happens before the event that may contribute to the behavior would fall into this category. When identifying the antecedents, consider where and when it is occurring, during what activity, with whom it occurred, and what any others were doing at the time.

For example, perhaps you are someone who finds yourself constantly arguing with your parents. You might realize that most of the time you don't even agree with what you're arguing with, but you do it anyway. You want to stop this behavior so you think about the last time it occurred. Set the scene first. In this situation: dinner at your parents' house, early afternoon, things were going fine, you were talking about your job and your career goals. This is the Antecedent.

Then we move onto the Behavior, which is the focus of this technique. This behavior can either be pivotal, which leads to further undesirable behaviors, or distracting, which can interfere with your own life or the lives of others. In this case, the behavior is uncontrollable anger, which is pivotal because it causes stress and irrationality in other parts of your life, too. It is important to describe the behavior in full when looking back in hindsight. In this situation, there are raised voices, dramatic gestures, insults thrown, and intentionally vicious comments being said, most of which were irrelevant to the actual argument.

Last is the Consequence of the behavior. This outcome is important because it is often one that reinforces the behavior. If the consequence is one that is genuinely undesirable, most unwanted behaviors will not be repeated, but if there is some sort of reward that is incidentally received, then the behavior will continue. In this case, the outcome may be that one of your parents, usually your mother, leaves the room upset and the dinner is cut short, whereby you then go home.

Now comes the analysis of the ABC. The Antecedent, as mentioned before, is the family dinner. It is important to mention the last thing to happen before the behavior. In this case, it was questions about career goals and aspirations. Already we have identified an important factor of the situation. Considering this is the last casual question before the argument, it is clear that this is the catalyst. If you are looking back at your own event and are able to identify the catalyst, consider why it affects you so much. Do you always react in the same way? If you can identify what it is that catalyzes a behavior you want to stop, then you can focus on it and actively try to redirect your behavior when you encounter a similar situation again.

The next thing to observe is the behavior itself. In this case, it is uncontrollable yelling, but it can be a whole range of different ones. Think about why it is that you choose this behavior. In this case, maybe you feel as if you're not being heard. Maybe you want to exercise some control or authority or overcompensate because you are feeling cornered. Whatever the reasoning behind it, think about if there is another way to release your emotions without that behavior. Even if it is something as simple as taking a moment to calm down, leaving the situation, or telling someone that you are not in an emotional state to continue. Find a way to redirect your emotions so that you produce a different behavior.

The last thing to consider is the consequence. If it is a recurring behavior, then that must mean you get some reward out of it. In this scenario, your mother has left the scene directly after the argument and you are forced to go home. Maybe this is exactly what you want—to spend less time with your parents. Maybe you just want them to support your career, and when it seems they aren't, then you don't wish to be there anymore.

Consider the outcomes after your own unfavorable behaviors. Are they what you actually desire? Do you only act in a certain way because you expect or anticipate a certain outcome? If this is the case, consider the outcome that you wish to achieve and think about how to achieve it in another way. If all you want is to be supported in your decisions, have a conversation that deals with this. If there is something you don't want to discuss, tell that person that there are things you would prefer to be off-limits that you might discuss when you're ready.

The ABC Loop is designed so that you can focus on the before and after of a behavior and figure out why certain behaviors are being repeated over and over again. If you can identify the catalyst and the outcome of a behavior, you can first stop the behavior when you recognize a similar setting, and then find a way to achieve the same desired outcome but in a more rational way.

Emotional Dashboarding

Emotional dashboarding is a very similar process to the ABC Loop. It also encourages stepping back from a situation to review your actions and reactions objectively, to "hack into your autopilot." While the introspective approach of emotional dashboarding is the same as the ABC Loop, there are a couple of more incremental steps:

SITUATION/ FACTS	THOUGHTS	EMOTIONS	BODILY SENSATIONS	IMPULSES/ ACTIONS
Example: Project due tomorrow	*"I don't feel like doing this." "I shouldn't have to."*	*Sadness, boredom, irritation*	*Heaviness, fatigue*	*Go to sleep, eat, space out*

Situation. Jot down the literal facts of the situation—details that couldn't be argued by any observer. This means leaving out opinions and existing prejudice or bias:

- A project is due tomorrow
- Your spouse's family is arriving for holidays
- You're assigned a new supervisor

- You've moved to a new place after a breakup and are invited to a party

Thoughts. Recall the personal interpretations and thoughts that went through your mind when the first feelings of distress or avoidance came up:

- "I don't feel like doing this," "I shouldn't have to"
- "Last year they seemed judgmental about the appearance of our house"
- "I've heard bad things about this person from people who've worked under him"
- "I'm not sure I'm ready to mingle with strangers in an unfamiliar place"

Emotions. Take a measure of the feelings you experienced during this conflict using only single emotion words:

- Sadness, boredom, irritation
- Resentment, disfavor, annoyance
- Anxiety, fear, concern
- Dejection, tension, uneasiness

When naming your reactions, ask yourself three times "why" these emotions came up.

The repetition of the question will encourage you to go as deep as possible to get to the root of the problem. In the first example, what mental picture caused the sadness about the late project—fear that it won't be good enough? Is the boredom because you feel it's a routine that keeps recurring? Are you irritated because there was a social event you would rather have done tonight?

Bodily sensations. Mark down the physical sensations you felt when experiencing the conflict:

- Heaviness, fatigue
- Stomach upset, headache
- Shoulder tension, increased heartbeat
- Lightness in head, slight tremors in hands

Be as literal as possible in describing bodily sensations. Avoid metaphors like "My heart was jumping out of my chest"—instead, say "I felt my heartbeat accelerating."

Impulses/actions. Write down your first instincts of what you wanted to do to relieve or avoid the conflict—things that made you feel good, distracted you, or minimized your attention to the preceding sensations:

- Go to sleep, eat, space out
- Watch TV, surf online
- Do "busy" work, make phone calls
- Drink alcohol, walk outside

This exercise makes us aware of what happens when we stray from the path of completing our goals. As with the "Emotions" component, ask yourself three times why these impulses came up.

Like the ABC Loop, the practice of emotional dashboarding develops a narrative that can be broken down and assessed like a fictional story. The dashboard adds a few internal elements—internal conflicts and physical sensations—that play the same role that "motivation" serves in fiction. Recognizing those alterations in your feelings and thoughts can help you identify them when they come up again.

One method may seem more appropriate than the other, depending on your circumstances. You may want to use the ABC Loop when initially coming across a conflict, and then the dashboard if it happens again or gets worse. If you sense your spouse's family being passive-aggressive or judgmental at your house for the first time, you may choose to run an ABC Loop first. If it happens again in another situation, you might want to run through the dashboard to see if you can gather additional insight about your moods and reactions.

It may simply be easier or more efficient just to execute an ABC Loop. Or perhaps your discomfort is so acute that you'd rather run the emotional dashboard. With honest self-inquiry, either method can help you make headway in discovering patterns and identifying troubling behaviors to change.

Name the Story

The bedtime stories we heard as children were usually very simplistic. There's a hero trying to accomplish a good deed with pure intent. There's some kind of villain who tries to thwart the hero, for no other reason than the villain *likes* evil. In most of these childhood tales, the heroes triumph, their perfect virtues being more than enough to derail the villains' wretchedness.

But as adults, the stories we read, or see on TV or in movies, aren't so quickly dissected. Heroes have more flaws or destructive tendencies—for example, the police lieutenant with a debilitating drinking problem. They can even morph into *antiheroes*: troubling characters from whom we hope to see some kind of humanity, like a mobster trying to keep his family alive.

Likewise, villains aren't all strictly defined by their badness. They could be doing very bad things (robbing banks) for reasons that would be noble if they were doing *positive* things (saving the family farm). Adult dramas are more complicated because the stories affect us only as we can relate them to our experiences as grown-ups.

We can borrow from dramatic structure for another powerful tool of detachment and evaluation: naming the story. This approach shows what emotions played a part, both in how we acted out the story *and* how we interpret or tell the story afterward.

The "victim or villain" exercise takes those two black-and-white opposites from children's storytelling:

Victim story—This version of events emphasizes your virtues, and absolves you of any responsibility for the things that happened.

Villain story—This account retells (and usually exaggerates) the faults and shortfalls of others, blaming their inherent evil nature for what happened.

Generally, if a situation is causing us distress, it's probably because we're retelling as a "victim" or "villain" story. Both make us feel unhappy or negative for different reasons. In victim stories, we're innocents that get taken advantageous of, regardless of our best intentions. In villain stories, other people are evil and have it in for us, regardless of what we do. And in both, we render our situations as "helpless"—we tell ourselves the situation's out of our control and just give up.

Let's take a basic scenario as an example: You've prepared and given a presentation for work in which you make a case for increasing your department's budget, but the people in charge didn't give you as much as you asked for.

The "victim" story: "I spent all night on these figures. I was honest and direct about why we needed them. I have a spotless record and work harder than anyone in my office. Everyone knows how loyal am I, and how pure my motivations are. Whatever the reason for their denying me, it's not my fault."

The "villain" story: "I gave a decent presentation, but those guys are hypocrites. They deny everyone else's budget requests but use company money for expensive dinners, drinks, and golf outings. They're selfish and irresponsible and they don't care about anyone but themselves. That's why they turned me down."

Parts of these stories could very well be true. Maybe you did work all night, and maybe they do use company money for entertainment. But fleshing these stories out may show something more complex at work behind our emotional responses.

That's where challenging the story comes in. This involves asking questions that will nudge you away from those starkly defined narratives. The "victim/villain" narrative always results in helplessness, which is passive—it leads to the idea that outcomes are foregone conclusions that we can't change. On the other hand, challenging the story can help the situation become clearer, and lead us into more *active* roles as change-makers.

In our presentation scenario above, you can get out of the victim mode by questioning your role: *"What am I pretending not to know about this situation?"* Maybe you knew that the company was temporarily cutting back on expenses, or that in the past you might have run over-budget on something else and are "under probation."

Similarly, you can transform the villains into the human entities they are: *"Why would reasonable, rational people do this?"* Perhaps they've forced budget cuts on their own departments as well. Maybe one of those company-funded dinners helped land a lucrative client that could turn the company's fortunes around.

After fleshing out the original victim-villain story with additional, humanizing details, you can get yourself out of helpless mode by asking, *"What's the right thing to do now to move toward what I really want?"* You might uncover that you need to brush up on your negotiation skills, or that you could work on showing a little less hubris. Or that someone on the panel offered constructive criticism, and you should schedule some time with them to talk it over.

Emotions in our personal and business relationships can often be outsized and difficult to examine objectively. But using the victim-villain-helpless exercise is effective, especially if we're honest in assessing the situations and ourselves.

Chapter 7. Perspective

When we speak of the merits of "emotional toughness," the term might be misinterpreted as "coldness and distance," or worse, "harshness and aggression." There are certainly cases in which efforts to maintain toughness have resulted in actions or statements that are aloof or abusive.

But the kind of toughness we're concerned with isn't something we direct toward others—it's about how we manage ourselves, how we rise to challenges or adversity, and how we persist. It doesn't harm our interpersonal relationships; in fact, it's something that actually improves how we connect and care for ourselves and others. Developing emotional toughness relies on objectivity and clarity, not bitterness or aggression.

In this chapter, we'll discuss two similar ways to develop and refine emotional toughness. Both have roots that go back thousands of years, so the fact that we're still talking about them speaks to their lasting influence. One was popularized by the famed philosopher-emperor Marcus Aurelius of ancient Rome, while the other was developed by the one and only Buddha. Both deal with how we perceive the emotional substance of our realities, and how regulating our feelings and temper are essential to experiencing a happy life. Additionally, they both work from the perspective of the "vast universe," and our place in that universe.

Buddhist Detachment

"Attachment is the origin, the root of suffering; hence it is the cause of suffering."
— The Dalai Lama, 1988

The tenets of detachment are in the first known volumes of Buddhist thought, the Pāli Canon. It's expressed as *nekkhamma*, which roughly translates to "renunciation." We often refer to this trait as "detachment," but it's perhaps more accurately expressed as "non-attachment."

Non-attachment isn't the same as deprivation. Consider food, for example: we have to eat to preserve ourselves, and there's nothing wrong with enjoying it. What non-attachment *does* address is desire and craving. It's logical to assume that when we cease dependence on certain life conditions, our odds of having a happier existence improve. We may still need it, but don't feel emotionally empty without it.

Dependence on External Things

We pin our internal happiness to external people, objects, and circumstances because of the feelings they bring us. We're conditioned to be that way. Getting material goods and emotional satisfaction feeds an internal sense of completion. Once we obtain those things or satisfy those desires, we tend to cling to them for dear life. We fear losing them, and stress out over that fear. We feel shattered if we lose something, or grieve when a situation changes. Breaking up, getting laid off, and losing a house or a car are major, traumatic events.

Our attachment to these feelings defines us. We feel euphoria over positive results and devastation over negative ones. Strangely, we depend on *both* those feelings, happy and sad, for our own comfort. Wallowing over regrets and disappointments can be a source of safety. The act of suffering can be as cozy and familiar as an easy chair. In trying to hold on to emotional habits, we restrict our ability to experience joy in the present.

When we stop trying to exercise control over the world around us, we actually set ourselves free. We give the world the freedom to fulfill us, and remove its power to destroy us. Letting go is letting happiness *in*.

This isn't a quick fix or a one-time decision. It's a commitment that must be deliberately renewed day to day, moment to moment. That in itself is the opposite of instant gratification, which is always temporary. It's something that must be cultivated, not just granted. It's a change to the way you experience and interact with the things and feelings you want.

The Problems with Attachment

Claiming that our unhappiness or depression is caused by attachment may still seem contradictory. Isn't getting what we want a good thing? Doesn't it drive us to work harder to achieve a physical level of comfort? Doesn't it reinforce our values?

Attachment plays a role in the conflicts over daily issues and occasional events. For example, arguments with others arise from our strict attachment to our opinions. When something doesn't go our way, we get angry because of our attachment to the results we want. When we lose something we cherish, we feel sad because we're no longer attached to those objects. Our agony over losing a loved one comes from their attachment to our lives.

This isn't a criticism of the emotions we feel toward people or things. Love, enjoyment, intelligence, and comfort are not disorders or adverse conditions. Rather, we're discussing the reliance itself—the fact that our peace of mind *depends* on fulfilling those needs, and our fixating on doing so.

Attachment to People

We may bristle at the suggestion that our attachment to *people* is an issue, but it's just as problematic. In fact, it could be *more* dangerous, because humans are more unpredictable and susceptible to change. We're driven by nature, and nature changes all the time.

Attachment to others is a bred condition, not something that occurs overnight. We develop feelings by spending time with someone. With partners, we gain affection; with coworkers, we build cooperation; with friends and family, we gain enjoyment and sentiment.

But in all those situations, we're not really attaching to the people—we're attaching to the *experience.* Our connection is with the emotions we feel when we're with them, good or bad. Our mind identifies pleasant sensations, so we crave them more often. But as those attachments grow and deepen, we start to nurture discomfort and fear losing those pleasures. We believe our happiness rests with their presence, and that leads us to think we need an outside factor to be contented. By doing so, we forfeit our own power to make ourselves happy.

Connection versus Entanglement

Attachment puts us in a state of need. Everything we do and think is focused on the thing we're attached to. Our perspective blurs, and our connections with others turn into entanglements.

When we experience connection, we share bonds and commonalities but maintain our individuality. Our over-attachment to the feelings we experience can distort that connection into codependency. We start thinking in terms of demands or needs. That's when we stop feeling connected, and begin feeling entangled.

We perceive external forces as things we need to be happy. But nothing outside of ourselves can truly bring happiness or security. The only ones in control of our own happiness are ourselves—our dependence on others might obscure that fact, but it doesn't change it.

As our attachments grow, our expectations become more fixed in our minds. Our fear of losing what we desire becomes more acute. We become concerned that the person or thing we're attached to may fall short of our needs, if not lost altogether. The experience can be painful.

When that worry manifests, our mind puts us in "survival mode." We become focused, obsessed, and maybe even addicted to the objects of our attachment. We become clingy, controlling, domineering, and insecure. Such emotions lead to near-dysfunction and disrupt our balance, and we act irrationally.

Pain and Suffering Is a Choice

We choose to experience misery and hurt. Believe it or not, that's good news.

We can avoid entanglement by living with non-attachment. That doesn't mean we withdraw or isolate ourselves from others, and never connect with anyone again. It doesn't mean we sacrifice our dreams or aspirations. It doesn't mean we devalue love, support, association, or compassion.

What it *does* mean is that we release our *need* for the relationship or thing that we've become attached to. We accept things as they are, and recognize that the situations in our existence will constantly evolve and change. Permanence is illusory—everything is temporary.

Accepting this viewpoint isn't automatic or easy. It requires letting go of details we feel strongly about but can't control. It's tough because our egos are constantly fed by the drive to *keep* that control. Releasing that need and putting our trust in the universe is a tough task.

When you can let go and practice healthy detachment, however, you can express truly unconditional love for your partner, and appreciate their presence in your life more honestly. You become more objective and focused. You operate at a higher level of productivity. Your relationships don't dissipate; they improve. They're harmonious, healthy, and passionate because you've freed yourself to have them. You can live life with more intensity and depth, and make sound decisions from a standpoint of wisdom and love.

Breaking Attachment

Detachment can be frightening, but it's much easier than it sounds. We don't just disengage with people or things—we merely change how we relate to them. Nobody feels *glad* about being dependent. Even if we claim to be happy, circumstances or events will arise that will expose that happiness as a fraud. Dependence only feels good when everything's going in our favor. When conditions change, or when people leave, that dependence becomes a source of anxiety.

Detachment relieves us of our expectations. Our happiness isn't based on need; it becomes authentic. We don't rely on things outside ourselves to make us happy because we're complete as we are. We can achieve happiness on our own. Happiness from outside factors becomes an *addition* to our positive state of mind, not the only source for it. The following steps can help you develop a healthy detachment that will inform and reinforce your life and relationships.

Awareness. Look at the attachments you have in your life—your partner, your surroundings, your social circles, or your work. Where have you given up power? Do you expect something from those relationships or things? Is any part of your connection controlled by your fear, anxiety, or insecurity? Find out which situations you might need to detach from.

Examination. Now that you've identified these attachments, inspect them more closely. What fuels your attachment? Do fear or insecurity play a part? How valid are your fears? If you sense they're irrational, then what are you *really* worried about? Take a lot of time with this step.

Acceptance. Accept each moment exactly for what it is. Don't compare or try to turn it to yesterday—that's gone. Don't try to extend the moment into something that will last forever, because it won't. Absorb the moment fully and enjoy it, because it will pass.

Now Is enough. Tomorrow will never be the same as today. Relationships will end; others will begin. Your surroundings will change. You'll be able to deal with those changes when they come. But right now, in the present moment, appreciate and enjoy what you have. No matter what the future holds, what you have now will always be enough.

Practice letting things be. Make peace with the moment. Don't worry something's wrong with you or your life. Operate from a standpoint of acceptance. This doesn't mean you can't work toward creating a better tomorrow or improving yourself. It just means accepting where you are now as the foundation for your achievements.

Release the need to know. Life will always be uncertain. Obsessing about tomorrow is self-defeating; there will always be another tomorrow after it. You can make projections and predictions about the future, and you might be right. But you can't affect them until they happen. The best way to be prepared is to work on what's before you right now.

Healthy Coping Mechanisms

Regardless of whether you believe in these philosophies, it's good to have healthy coping mechanisms to regulate our feelings. Achieving inner peace or Zen is a great thing, but realistically you can't depend on them all the time. Sometimes you may have to work off some steam.

Coping is a response to physical or psychological stress triggered by change. It's an important part in maintaining health and emotional well-being. Coping mechanisms can be enacted as behaviors, thoughts, or emotions that help you adapt to the shifts in your life.

Most stressors are defined as negative events: death of a loved one; sexual, physical, or emotional trauma or abuse; loss of a job; divorce. But positive events, like a new job or marriage, can also increase stress levels, and need just as much coping skills as negative ones. Anything that sparks a change needs to be monitored and managed through coping.

Different ways of coping. Your set of stressors is unique. What affects you might not affect the person next to you. As such, researchers divide coping mechanisms into two broad categories: instrumental coping or problem-solving, and emotion-focused coping. **Instrumental coping** focuses on ways to decrease the stress level coming from a specific situation—the factors or conditions that might be causing pressure. **Emotion-focused** coping takes an inward view, and maintains emotional fitness during demanding times.

Coping is also labeled as *active* or *avoidant*. Active coping approaches the stressful situation head-on to try to stop a negative outcome. Avoidant coping, simply put, is ignoring the problem at hand and taking actions that reinforce one's denial of the problem.

Mechanisms for coping come in a few different styles and categories:

Diversion. Diversions are avoidant, but not always bad. They give us time off from obsessing over the problem, which can be necessary to keep us safe and sane. Diversions are never intended to *solve* a problem, though. You'll eventually have to get back to it.

But diversions can be beneficial. Taking up arts and crafts, watching movies or television, playing games, reading, cleaning the house, surfing the web, and going for a walk are diversions that offer relief from our most immediate stress—and can also add meaningful context to our lives.

Social and interpersonal coping. Scientific studies assert that social occasions can counteract the effects of stress on our DNA. They can be as intimate as a phone call or discussion with a close friend or loved one. They can be external as a night out with friends, or taking part in a huge group discussion.

Tension release and catharsis. This more dramatic coping mechanism allows us to "act out" strong emotions in ways that don't harm ourselves or others. Examples include primal scream, punching into a pillow, boxing lessons, or squeezing a stress ball. One should, however, take caution to not let that release become a habit that could affect our real lives. If you punch a pillow and picture someone's face on it, don't extend that method to an attack on the actual person you're thinking about.

Exercise. The physical benefits of exercise are obvious, but a workout or jog can also produce endorphins, which in turn promote a calm or euphoric feeling.

Spiritual coping. This kind of stress management does not need to be tied to a religious belief system. Prayer, meditation, communing with nature, or working for a worthy cause can satisfy our need to feel worthwhile. Development of spiritual well-being answers to our drive for a sense of purpose. Transcendental meditation, guided relaxation, and chanting are ways to center ourselves; volunteering for a charity or public work efforts can answer our need to feel useful.

Limit-setting. Although we've discussed setting limits as a preventative measure, it's also a way to decrease stress. Saying no when you're too busy to help someone, stopping participation in work activities that don't fit your skill set, or holding back access by people in tense situations that don't involve you all help your survival. Setting limits may require some negotiations, but restricting new avenues of tension is as important as dealing with the existing ones.

Stoic Thought

Buddhism can be hard to digest, but the essential idea is very similar to that of Stoicism. Stoicism is a way of viewing life and seeing your place in the world, and it was originally put into words by the Athenian philosopher Zeno around the third century BCE.

Stoic philosophy argues that unchecked emotions are some of the biggest enemies of your happiness and fulfillment. Rationality, perspective, and practicality are what drive Stoicism.

According to Stoicism, you have the utmost free will in any circumstance, regardless of what your emotions might tell you. There is your *emotional* reality and the *objective* reality, and you can choose which you want to abide by. You have more control of what's going on in your life than you realize.

There are many ways to characterize Stoicism, but I find it best to break it into two primary tenets.

The first important tenet of Stoicism that will seek to promote emotional resilience is that everything that happens in the world is neutral—every event and consequence thereof. Every event has a different effect on everyone, but the events themselves are neutral, without intent, and play no favorites. There is no bad or good; it is all subjective. It is created with you, along with all emotions and judgments.

This means that it's your reaction and perception that cause your unhappiness. If you perceive events to be negative, they will be negative. If they perceive them to be positive, you will find the positive in them.

If you are sitting in a café and a car slams into your parked car on the street outside, you have a choice about how you will respond. It's a neutral event, and you can attach any set of emotions to it you want.

You can react the way most people do and freak out or play the victim, or you can calmly take out your phone and solve the problem by researching new cars with upgraded sound systems. The operative facts are the same, yet two very different outcomes will ensue. Which reaction do you think will lead to a more orderly resolution of what just happened?

No matter how you react, the facts will remain the same: your car is going to need repairs, or will need to be replaced.

Your emotional stability hinges upon your reaction and perception of neutral events, which every event is. It's your response and opinion about the event that either causes you tremendous emotional distress, or leads you to a quick resolution with minimal stress. Taking ownership of your role in your level of happiness and stability is why the same event can affect people in drastically different ways.

What makes things negative, unpleasant, and stressful is our judgment of those otherwise neutral events. We don't have control over most of the situations we are put into, despite our best efforts. You can't control other people or the weather—if you feel that you do, you are fighting a losing battle because you are setting yourself up for continual disappointment. But we do have control over 100% of our reactions and responses to those situations. This is a process that can make or break your mood and perception of life.

People react in predictable ways when things they perceive to be negative happen. They either blame someone else, or they beat themselves up emotionally. Because of that lack of control over events, many are frustrated by their feelings of helplessness. Focus instead on how you respond to what's taking place right now in your life.

Outside forces are not out to make you miserable. Even if they are, you are making the choice to feel that emotion. Look within.

The world hands us a blank slate every morning; you are the sole writer and editor of what is written on that slate. Some people will inevitably see the silver lining of a storm cloud, while others are overwhelmed by the smallest hint of darkness. Which will you be?

The second tenet of Stoicism is to always temper your expectations and expect difficulty and challenge. This isn't necessarily about being pessimistic; it's more about being realistic and steeling yourself for the hardships you'll encounter. It's amazing what adjusted expectations can do for your outlook: how would you feel if you won the lottery and expected to versus if you won the lottery and forgot you had even bought a ticket?

Many of us are waking up with the former expectation—that life will or should deliver us something. It's a dangerous place to be. When you can move away from this thinking and ask yourself, "What's the worst that can happen?" you'll be prepared and unsurprised. As you may have surmised, Stoicism is a particularly helpful tool in battling the obstacles we face in our lives.

Going a step further, you can, as the Stoics say, *turn the obstacle upside down*. Train yourself to avoid judging events as purely good or bad. In fact, realize you can even turn all obstacles upside down, looked at through another perspective, to suit your purposes. This means that anything that seems to present an obstacle should actually be seen as an opportunity for something positive and growth-oriented.

The most practical effect is enabling the sufferer (so to speak) to become immune to negative emotional spirals. Instead, they force themselves to engage in alternative thought patterns to gain perspective and move forward rationally.

For example, imagine you are a nurse and you have a patient who is very cranky. The reason you approached this person is because you wanted to help them. But this person is being surly, doesn't want to cooperate, or even tries to bully you. In short, this person is being mean and nasty.

According to Stoics, instead of feeling hassled, or feeling that this person is making your life difficult, try to think of this person as actually helping you out. How can that be? Well, this person's behavior is giving you a tremendous opportunity to exercise new virtues that you should have more of in your life, like being understanding, patient, and compassionate.

Another example drawn from Stoic teachings is the death of a loved one. If you love somebody, it's easy to fall into despair when they pass away. But you could use this loss as an opportunity to show fortitude. Instead of feeling pain and loss, you can look at this commonly negative situation as an opportunity to practice inner strength, calm, control, equanimity, and level-headedness.

Our life is full of teachable moments, like the parables of old or Aesop's Fables. Regardless of how negative a particular event may seem, you can always try to reinterpret it as a positive opportunity or look at the other side of the situation.

The more you turn the obstacle upside down, the more you'll realize that there really is no such thing as good and bad. It all depends on how you choose to perceive something.

For centuries, Stoicism has been a virtual antidote for emotional disruptions that can plague any of us. It tells you that you unequivocally have the power to create your own reality. Meanwhile, Buddhist principles also make it clear that your surroundings don't need to change for change to occur. Your mental states are freer than you think, and sometimes a mental switch is all it takes for resilience to spring forth.

Chapter 8. Safeguarding Tactics

Improving your emotional response and coping mechanisms will always be effective. But for everyday life, it's best to have some strategies that aren't necessarily developed in crisis mode. Taking preventative measures will keep you healthy and grounded, and form a solid foundation that eases the strain of emergencies.

Gratitude

We associate the emotion of gratitude with positive outcomes. Although the adage of being grateful for what we have is well-known, it's not always a practice we grasp, even though there's *always* something to be grateful for. Still, studies have shown that just being aware of or questioning your gratitude—even if you can't think of anything off the top of your head—can effect some powerful chemical changes.

For example, stop reading for a minute and consider five things you're grateful for. They don't need to be big accomplishments or achievements; they can be simple parts of everyday living. "I have clean air to breathe," "I have family and friends who love me," "I have a place to sleep," "I live in interesting times."

You might not have noticed any immediate changes, but you may have just helped yourself by uttering or thinking about those affirmations. Many scientists contend that gratitude can be a natural antidepressant. Thinking about or asking what you're grateful for actually activates certain neural circuits, which produce dopamine and serotonin, neurotransmitters that regulate our pleasure centers and mood levels. They then travel the neural byways to the "bliss" center of the brain, much like a prescribed antidepressant. The more you stimulate them, the stronger and more automatic they become.

Hebb's Law states, "Neurons that fire together wire together." We see this proverb at work in everyday life. When you're walking through a forest for the first time, you're forging a new path that can provide challenges. But the more the path is traveled, the more defined and easier to follow it becomes.

So it works with the human brain. The more a neural pathway is activated, the less effort it takes to animate it the next time. Since the practice of mental gratitude greases the neurons, simple, short daily meditations on your appreciation can actually ease your tension on a biological level.

Dopamine, in particular, is extraordinarily useful in attitude enhancement. It's called the "reward" neurotransmitter because it feels good to get. But it also helps initiate action, and increasing it makes you more likely to do whatever made you happier. It's like the brain saying, "That thing you just did? Yeah, do that again!"

The downside is that negative thought patterns activate *their* neural pathways as well. When we constantly see the negative aspects of a situation and seek out problems, the neural paths for negative thinking grow stronger. Proactively applying gratitude can train our brains to seek out constructive elements in our lives, while lessening the destructive ones. We water the flowers instead of watering the weeds.

Researchers Robert A. Emmons and Michael E. McCullough performed a study in 2003 called "Counting Blessings Versus Burdens: An Experimental Investigation of Gratitude and Subjective Well-Being in Daily Life." They gathered a group of young adults and told them to keep journals. One group was instructed to write daily entries of things they were grateful for, and the other was told to write about their annoyances or why they were better off than other people.

The researchers' instructions to the gratitude journalists encouraged them to note any facet of their lives that they were grateful for, regardless of importance: "There are many things in our lives, both large and small, that we might be grateful about. Think back over the past week and write down on the lines below up to five things in your life that you are grateful or thankful for."

For journalists who were given the task of writing down their annoyances, the researchers said, "Hassles are irritants—things that annoy or bother you. They occur in various domains of life, including relationships, work, school, housing, finances, health, and so forth. Think back over today and, on the lines below, list up to five hassles that occurred in your life." The results were predictably persuasive. The gratitude journalists showed greater increases in determination, attention, enthusiasm, and energy. Their findings showed gratitude to be a powerful social and spiritual accelerator:

> *The experience of gratitude, and the actions stimulated by it, build and strengthen social bonds and friendships. Moreover, encouraging people to focus on the benefits they have received from others leads them to feel loved and cared for by others... Therefore, gratitude appears to build friendships and other social bonds. These are social resources because, in times of need, these social bonds are wellsprings to be tapped for the provision of social support. Gratitude, thus, is a form of love, a consequence of an already formed attachment as well as a precipitating condition for the formation of new affectional bonds... Gratitude is also likely to build and strengthen a sense of spirituality, given the strong historical association between gratitude and religion... Finally, to the extent that*

> *gratitude, like other positive emotions, broadens the scope of cognition and enables flexible and creative thinking, it also facilitates coping with stress and adversity.*

Just as tellingly, the study proved that realizing that other people were worse off does *not* equal gratitude. Rather, gratitude is an appreciation of the positive aspects of your own situation.

Emmons's and McCullough's findings could inspire you to try journaling yourself. Putting your thoughts in writing is almost always a good practice.

Start out by replicating the exercise at the beginning of this chapter: write down five things that you're grateful for. Make a conscious effort to reflect upon the things that bring you joy, elation, or peace of mind. As we've said, there's *always* something to be thankful for in a given situation.

Commit to this practice every day for the next 10 days. Keep a journal by your bed, and take a minute before sleeping to recall the events of the day that made you smile. Or start a list on your smartphone to write pleasant events down as they happen (also a nice way for a quick pick-me-up when you're not having a great day). You can also find an "accountability partner" to keep a list like yours. Every week you can check in for five minutes, and read your lists to each other.

This practice can turn gratitude into your own mental gym—strength training for your neural pathways. The more you practice the act of gratitude, the healthier that muscle gets. Just like in physical gyms, the more you show up and work the gratitude angle, the easier the workouts get.

If writing feels like too much, you can ease into gratitude practice with an extremely uncomplicated daily exercise: every time your feet hit the ground after you get out of bed, simply say thank you. Nature likes to be appreciated and paid attention to the same way as humans. Acknowledging nature helps our own lives bloom in response.

We get used to whatever situations surround us without much effort. Initiating gratitude in all walks of our own lives might be a more trying task, or even impractical in certain situations. When was the last time you turned the key in your car's ignition and praised the miracles of the internal combustion engine? Have you ever taken a walk through a city park and expressed thanks for arch supports? Do you take time from work to appreciate the craft and convenience of your hole punch or stapler?

But in truth, those are all perfectly fine things to be grateful for—especially when we don't have them. Natural disasters like hurricanes or earthquakes can give effected people a new appreciation for things like running water and electricity. It's true that nothing should be taken for granted—but realistically, that feeling doesn't necessarily last for long. A few days removed from those disasters, you're back to cursing the elevator if it takes more than 30 seconds to get to your floor.

The central point is that gratitude is easy to execute, but not always easy to maintain. There's nothing wrong about expressing annoyances over little inconveniences, but letting those irritations inform the core of our beings is ill-advised. We've seen how our brain transforms itself based on even our smallest impulses. If we can make gratitude a more constant and consistent impulse, our brains will see to it that our happiness improves.

Journaling

Keeping journals is a part of almost any facet of modern life you can think of—business, art, information-gathering, and of course news. It's not a stretch to understand its service in maintenance of ourselves and our mental health. A couple of organized journal techniques are particularly helpful.

“Worry journals” are an element of cognitive behavior therapy (CBT), a long-time aid in treating emotional disorders. They’ve also been used in sleep therapy for subjects who experienced anxiety. The goal of the worry journal is to air out our worries, fears, anxieties, and issues on paper throughout the course of the day.

One method of worry journaling involves writing one’s concerns or fears on the left-hand side of a page, thinking about how to resolve them, and writing these plans on the right-hand side. The writer then closes the journal, and at least tries not to think about the worries until the next day when, theoretically, some of the plans can be executed.

Researchers from Pennsylvania State University decided to see whether worry journaling alone could improve the emotional balance of subjects. They recruited 51 patients with various forms of anxiety disorder. From this pool, certain subjects were randomly selected to keep a worry journal for 10 days. Those remaining were told to keep a journal in which they simply recorded their thoughts. The researchers also text-messaged participants at random times during the day, prompting them to write immediately.

After the 10-day experiment ended, those with worry journals were asked to review how many of their worries had actually come true. Most of them–91%–hadn't. The brief text interventions were enough to significantly reduce their anxiety levels, more so than those who had simply kept thought journals. Thirty days after the experiment concluded, the worry journal group was still performing better than the control group.

An interesting finding of the Penn State study was how quickly the worry journal participants manifested positive changes, even after only 10 days. By documenting their worries, fears, obstacles, and predictions, they made progress in reorienting themselves to the present—not the future, where some of their biggest anxieties lay. "It may also make the worthlessness of engaging in excessive catastrophic expectations more apparent," the researchers said.

These results support the idea that putting our self-inventories on record can be effective in managing stress. Worry journaling could be a beneficial part of your regular response to stress and daily routine.

For example, let's say that your business has lost its biggest customer, or that you've had a contentious argument with an employee. In frustration, you walk into your office and shut the door. Your emotions aren't controllable—you're upset, angry, maybe even frightened of the fallout.

To regain your emotional balance, you focus on your breathing for a few moments. Then you open your journal. You write down exactly what's upsetting you, what you're worried about, and what your biggest obstacles, problems, or fears are. You must be honest—understand that nobody except you will read this journal unless you give it to them.

Some experts suggest writing in your journal every single day. That's certainly not a bad idea, but sometimes life intrudes upon our ability to do that. We don't always have time. Other days we *do* have time, but don't feel like we have anything significant to say.

But in moments of worry, anxiety, or upset, we *always* have something to say, and plenty of it. Keeping it bottled up may prevent us from doing anything else until we finally express our frustrations, so that's a good reason to write it down in the journal on the spot.

These situations illustrate a good practice when it comes to journaling: *follow your emotional prompts.* Writing during times when we're scared, angry, or upset might not be the first action you'll think of taking, but it can go a long way in addressing your immediate emotional needs. By the time you're done, you might be at least a little glad you did, and chances are the next time writing *will* be the first action you take.

The journal is where you dump your frustrations, problems, and concerns. Keep writing and until you've finally written everything you need to say. Remember, the journal's a "safe zone" and you're not obligated to share it with anyone. It's where you can be direct, unsparing, and honest, without unforeseeable repercussions.

Two outcomes will probably emerge from documenting your feelings. While writing, you'll gradually become calmer and less upset. You may start to see solutions to your problems come forth. Laying your problem out in words on the page makes a future course of action appear and helps you figure out what to do.

Make "Stop" and "It's Okay To" Lists

Journaling is free-flowing and open-ended, but another approach that could be helpful involves making two lists that are very specific in what they accomplish.

STOP:

- Putting yourself last
- Trying to be all things to all people
- Being afraid to say no or yes
- Talking down to yourself
- Depending on others to make you happy
- Letting outside events define you
- Settling for less
- Limiting beliefs
- Keeping score in games you don't need or can't win

IT'S OKAY TO:

- Ask for help
- Be constantly changing
- Not always be linearly improving
- Admit vulnerability and weakness
- Not be invulnerable
- Be knocked down and feel hopeless
- Cry
- Speak up for what you value
- Question the rules of the games you play

"Stop" and "It's Okay To" lists serve as daily affirmations of your values. They remind you what's acceptable and what's not, what boundaries you have set up, and what brings you closer to your goals. They're also empowering—they give you self-generated, unequivocal directions. "Stop" items are things you should hold yourself back from; "It's Okay To" items list out what's acceptable.

Write out these lists and post them in a place you see regularly. They'll serve as guidelines that will keep you on course to a life of emotional strength and wellness. See the following example:

After making these lists, we can incorporate their contents into internal action when we have a conflict. Since they are based on the values *we* define for ourselves, the hope is that these principles will be easier to stick to when a such a situation arises.

For example, someone in your extended family comes to you with an investment opportunity. They've had a difficult time staying afloat as an adult, and have been bailed out once or twice after making some unwise credit decisions. You mistrust their judgment about financial matters. But since they're family, you let them talk to you, and you listen completely to their pitch.

While they seem earnest about the opportunity, you have doubts that it's anything more than a pyramid scheme, and you say so. The family member becomes angry and accuses you of being closed off to new ideas and "going against the family." You attempt to explain your position more patiently, but before you finish they angrily stomp out. You feel some amount of guilt, possibly some shame as a result.

Let's use the above "Stop/It's Okay To" lists to back up your reactions (your personal lists may be different, but for this example, we'll use ours). Your instincts told you to reject your family member's latest plan, and they responded negatively. One of the "Stop" items was "Being afraid to say no." Perhaps you have a tendency to help as many of your friends or family as you can, which is impossible to fulfill. But another "Stop" item is "Trying to be all things to all people." In this scenario, you've successfully prevented those acts from happening.

What about the "It's Okay To" list? You explained your reasons for not agreeing to invest in a patient manner. That could answer a couple of items on the "It's Okay To" list: "Speak up for what you value," and possibly "Take time to determine your feelings about a situation." You explained why taking on this dubious investment goes against your needs and principles, but only after you also let them finish so you could hear them fairly.

After the conflict ended, you might have felt guilty or ashamed. But you acted according to the ground rules you set forth in that list, which are completely reasonable and came from your own self-questioning. Knowing that you stuck to your own self-defined principles may not make you feel better *immediately*—but probably much sooner than you would have if you *didn't* stick to them.

Again, your personal list will likely vary from our example. You should have some items unique to your own experience, and that's what makes the lists invaluable. Mistakes, regrets, and even accidents can happen when we forget or work against our belief systems and values. These lists are one way to keep them near the forefront of our attention, and though they won't eradicate all conflict from our lives, they could help us navigate them with more assurance.

Chapter 9. Preventative Care is the Best Care

As discussed in Chapter 1, the brain maintains a strong negativity bias. It's not an entirely destructive force. Our continued survival depends on our ability to keep harmful elements at bay as much as possible—dangerous encounters, food one is allergic to, toxic people or situations to avoid, and so forth. But because neural activity in response to negative signals is so strong, it can cease being an effective survival mechanism and become an obstacle to your sense of resiliency and overall happiness.

Knowing and reminding ourselves that our brains work that way is part of the battle. Therefore, part of the battle in staying strong with your emotions is to actively battle this instinct and generate your own positivity.

To a lot of us, that's no small task. Negativity is more accumulative than positivity, piling up in the psyche with seemingly little effort. It's easy for the brain to lie back and let fears, terrors, and anxieties unfold one after the other. When they get to a certain mass, negativity bias starts to feel like an anchor that can't be overcome.

Many of us tend to characterize positivity as something that requires more labor, an exhaustive act that might not even make a significant dent in our negativity in the end. But in reality, positivity is a force that pays off even when we take small steps to bring it about. It's far easier to inject positivity into our lives and emotions than our negativity will have us think.

Give Yourself Small Things

In 2008, psychologists Leif D. Nelson and Tom Meyvis conducted a study on "Interrupted Consumption." Its goal was to assess how our experiences are affected by pauses in pleasure—for example, whether an ice cream cone is more enjoyable if you're prevented from eating one for a period of time. Nelson and Meyvis theorized that temporarily stopping an enjoyable activity intensifies or heightens the satisfaction we get from it.

Participants in the study all received three-minute massages in specially designed chairs. One group received continuous massages for the entire time, and the other group got a 20-second break in the middle of their sessions. Afterward, the participants were asked to rate their massage experience.

The group that received the break in the middle of their massage reported more positive results. They were more "willing to pay twice as much to repeat the experience," and "almost twice as much to purchase the massage cushion." The participants' expectations that the break would detract from the massage proved to be incorrect; Nelson and Meyvis's hypothesis that the break would "enhance the experience" turned out to be right.

The results demonstrated that pausing a pleasurable experience prevents the subjects from becoming acclimatized or accustomed to it. Nelson and Meyvis described this effect as "intensifying." The contrast between the moment of no stimulus and the resumption of the massage made the overall experience more satisfying than a nonstop massage.

A takeaway from this study is that adaptation is the enemy of happiness. Getting used to positive sensations gradually takes away the pleasure we derive from them. Eventually we may not even consider these experiences as pleasant anymore: they simply become an expected routine we take for granted. Having a break in the stimulation, on the other hand, makes us appreciate our enjoyment more.

Taking a greater number of smaller, different satisfactions could give us more pleasure than larger ones. Acts that give us physical or provisional gratifications—having a midday sweet treat, or a taking a quick shopping trip—can qualify as miniature rewards in which we can take pleasure. Always having something to look forward to, no matter how small, has a marked effect on your positivity. This is even stronger if it has to be interrupted and continued over a series or days or even weeks.

Small pleasures aren't strictly tied to food and purchasing power. Recognizing contentment in modest breaks in our routines can help us develop relief and exhilaration in more active or mental pursuits. It sharpens and broadens our appreciation of the humble satisfactions—walking in nature, viewing art, reading an amusing story, play-acting with a child—that are regularly accessible to us. There are a few simple steps we can take to unlock our abilities to enjoy simple pleasures.

Keep self-aware. This step is common to almost all types of self-improvement, but it's especially useful for simple pleasures. Take time to focus on yourself and your needs, and make a wish list of the things you want to experience. You have the knowledge that negativity is everywhere, and yet positivity can be so easy to attain if you are strategic.

Schedule your enjoyment. One common barrier to having joyful encounters is the pressure we feel from not having enough time. Being proactive about setting up a schedule is a good way to overcome this obstacle. Start a calendar and reserve some time exclusively for relaxing. This is what you will anticipate and what will keep you afloat in tough times. Keep track of the time you're spending on your various responsibilities and engagements, and find spare moments or stretches when you can give yourself something to enjoy.

Budget your activity. In addition to simply making time for experiences, it's important to be attentive to the *kind* of experiences we have. Reduce activities that clutter your mind or breed gloom—especially watching too much news, overusing the Internet, or any other passive activity that only interrupts boredom. Concentrate your efforts and money toward having *experiences* rather than possessions. What hobbies do you want to engage in, but never do? Who do you want to spend time with, but always forget to? Be deliberate and thoughtful about the choices you make, and seek pursuits that make you more physically and mentally involved.

Develop more satisfying relationships. Just as cutting more harmful relationships from our lives helps us heal, improving the positive ones we have helps us grow in our quest for happiness. Making a point to meet new people is a great way to expand our experiences. Caring for our existing friendships can help, too. Practice the art of listening to others, and allow yourself to speak your mind back. Work on listening in the spirit of compassion and empathy. Make the effort to express appreciation—over-thanking is always better than not thanking at all.

Try new things. Many of us feel nervous about the unknown, and that's why diving into new experiences can be transformative. Get outside to better appreciate your immediate surroundings. Take a small day trip to a convenient locale you've never been to. It's never been easier to teach yourself how to do something new: cooking unfamiliar cuisines, creating arts and crafts, learning how to make small home repairs. Accept and embrace the idea of always being in learning mode—open yourself up to new insights, even with experiences you have all the time. Routine can be boring, while the simple novelty of something unfamiliar can bring amazing excitement.

Allow yourself to express happy emotions. Most of us need no prompting to feel disappointment or depression, but many have difficulty acknowledging when we're feeling joy or contentment. Give yourself permission to experience happiness. It's not cheesy, corny, or self-indulgent. Make a point to celebrate and commemorate your moments of bliss, victory, or contentment—record them, take pictures, or just speak your pleasant thoughts into a recorder. Everything matters—perhaps not on a real-life level, but they accumulate within your psyche and drastically change the narrative you can tell yourself. At the very least, when we're overtaken with dark moments, try to remember and affirm that all such feelings are temporary—"this too shall pass."

Savor the Joys You Have

Studies have also been conducted to understand the benefits of *savoring*—the mental and emotional act of appreciation of a particular experience.

One such study investigated a group of depressed participants who were asked to take their time and relish an activity they normally hurry to get through. The activities were all part of their daily functions: eating a meal, taking a shower, finishing a work assignment, or walking to a subway or bus stop. The subjects were told to write down how they felt after extending these routines, and how those feelings compared to those when they rushed through them.

Another study surveyed members of a community that were comparatively healthy in their states of mind. These participants were told to savor two pleasant experiences each day, simply by reflecting on them for two to three minutes and trying to make the pleasure last as long and intensely as possible.

The results for both studies were dramatic: taking time to savor certain events, even ones normally associated with routine and tasks, increased the participants' overall happiness and decreased their depression to some extent. The simple act of slowing down and being intentional with their actions improved how they felt about, well, everything.

The Journal of Positive Psychology noted that these and other findings supported the theory that "savoring responses are an important mechanism by which individuals transmute the raw stuff of daily life into positive effect."

In other words, savoring in itself is a pleasurable activity. Savoring is a way to add and reinforce another layer of emotional benefit to an act of pleasure, on top of the sensual and mental enjoyment that such acts provide.

Taking time to finish and appreciate a meal or dessert is an obvious example of physical savoring, but it's not the only one. Focusing, even meditating, on the character and nature of things we do and see ramp up the benefits as well. Viewing human drama from a park bench, experiencing the rush of breeze and motion in a bike ride, noting the give and take in a group conversation with friends—all are activities that can be transformed by stretching them out and appreciating each part.

Reflecting and communicating our appreciation of these experiences is another way to savor them after the fact. Whether one writes their thoughts down in a blog, talks about their experience to friends, or merely meditates and gives thanks privately adds another, deeper level to the episodes that make up our lives. The act of savoring can lead to a more conscious state of mind in which we have clearer, sharper interactions with the world, and find more to appreciate about it.

Create Anticipation

It's probably easy to understand the gratification we receive from experiences or objects that we have. But is it possible to reap an emotional profit from something we *don't yet* have?

Cornell psychology scientist Thomas Gilovich and his colleagues ran a series of tests in 2014 on the subject of anticipation. The team asked nearly 100 students to think about a purchase they were planning to make "in the very near future." Gilovich divided these purchases into two types: "experiential" and "material." Experiential purchases were identified as those "made with the primary intention of acquiring a life experience"; material ones were those made to obtain tangible objects.

Gilovich asked his subjects to rate their anticipation of the purchases on a scale ranging from impatience to excitement. They were then asked to share how pleasant their anticipation felt on a scale from "extremely unpleasant" to "extremely pleasant."

The results backed up the Gilovich team's speculation that anticipation of an *experience* was more pleasant than one of future material gain. Similarly, the subjects reported more levels of excitement in regard to experiential purchases, and more impatience when it came to material ones. It didn't matter if it actually came to fruition or not; the act of anticipating was a pleasurable exercise in itself.

There's a lot to learn from this study. Experiences are generally more transformative than material objects, and therefore probably more attuned to our emotional responsiveness. Week-long holidays, day trips, and leisure or physical activities feed our mentality, senses, and imaginations more directly—whereas obtaining a material object is more associated with the filling of a need or desire. It's likelier for one to look forward to a trip to a ski resort, rather than to a sporting goods store.

There are less definitions and concrete expectations to a future experience. Uncertainty, unpredictability, and adventure are usually valued aspects of those kinds of events, whereas in our material goods, we favor reliability and consistency. We may know what we're *planning* on doing when we go on vacation—but we don't know conclusively how it's going to feel until we do it.

Material purchases also induce a certain competitive aspect. In consumerist society, many people with disposable income approach the accumulation of material goods from the perspective of "keeping up with the Joneses"—making sure that they don't fall too far behind their neighbors or friends in amount and quality of personal possessions. Think of the feeding frenzies that often happen at discount department stores on Black Friday after Thanksgiving. Experiences, on the other hand, emphasize the feeling, the sensation, and the creation of memories, all reflecting our individual ideals of contentment and elation. Having something to anticipate generates a host of positive emotions, and promotes a greater connection with life and the delights it can offer.

Anticipation isn't perceived as something we can necessarily affect or manage ourselves; it's something that just happens. It's why sometimes planning a trip is more fun than the actual trip itself—you get the opportunity to fantasize and dream about how amazing it just might be. There are a few small measures that help create a healthy sense of anticipation on a daily basis, and even enhance the experience when it happens.

Fill your schedule. Of course, this is a combination of the phenomenon of anticipation and how small things tend to keep us lighter in mood. We all look forward to the weekend when we have a big party planned, so why not replicate that feeling on a more frequent or even daily basis? Fill your schedule with things to anticipate, people to see, and events to attend. They don't have to be expensive, and you can do them alone. What's important is that you simply have something on the calendar that allows you to imagine how nice it will be. The event itself might be mediocre, but that only lasts two hours. Your anticipation can last over a week—over 100 hours. That's a favorable trade-off.

Plan your experience. If you're going on a road trip, what will the day be like? What time will you get up? What towns will you pass through? What music will you play in the car? If you're cooking a meal with food you're not familiar with, where can you get the ingredients? Is there a specialty store you can go to that's different from your usual supermarket?

Most of us, of course, make plans for experiences we're going to undertake, but a lot of the details are "grunt work." By being a little more creative about the flow and process, you can look forward to more than the actual experience. Working on those details could also unlock the pleasure for more small things, like we've already discussed. The more you immerse yourself in the experience beforehand, the greater the pleasure will be.

Learn about your experience. Beyond planning the day, you can find out more intangible details about your upcoming event. What's the history of the town you're going to visit on your road trip? Are there any entertaining interviews with the musician you're planning to see in concert? What are some of the hidden strategies in fly-fishing that you can use on your trip to the river? Learning about the peripheral points of your event gives you a new angle to look for when you're actually experiencing it, and helps to expand your curiosity in general.

Visualize your experience. Take a few moments to meditate on how the motion will feel on the slopes when you're skiing on them. Try to imagine how the kitchen will smell when you're cooking for your dinner party. Think about how you'll talk to the friend you haven't seen in years who's coming into town for a visit.

"Dreaming" about how a future event will feel is something we almost automatically do anyway. Concentrating on how our senses will react on a more minute level will heighten our expectations. But remember, even if a couple of those visualizations don't actually manifest during the event, the surprise over what *does* happen will naturally enrich our enjoyment and meaning.

What we've described in this chapter are fairly easy, quietly proactive approaches that reveal their benefits over time. They can stimulate healthy enthusiasm and improve our outlooks. The small gifts we give ourselves, the deliberate savoring of what we have, and an anticipation of future experience can develop qualities of optimism, hope, and passion for the lives we lead. They won't make our problems magically evaporate, or remove all our disappointments—but they *can* make such moments easier to withstand, and amplify our joy and value for the good things.

Chapter 10. Emotional Self-Defense

That didn't happen.
And if it did, it wasn't that bad.
And if it was, that's not a big deal.
And if it is, that's not my fault.
And if it was, I didn't mean it.
And if I did, you deserved it.
- **The Narcissist's Prayer**

Preventative care is important, but what might be even more important is to train yourself to defend against those who are actively trying to undermine your emotional resilience and actually prefer you unstable. This is when you must proactively establish self-defense from others, whereas the rest of this book has been about defeating your own demons and defending from yourself.

I'm talking about those would who seek to hurt, manipulate, control, or use you for their own purposes. Emotional manipulation is a tricky subject to discuss. To a certain degree, all human beings are manipulative. Our struggles to survive, our opportunities for advancement, and even our efforts to improve the human condition all occasionally rely on our abilities to shape and mold the opinions of others.

Manipulation, though it has a sinister undertone, isn't even always negative or unwanted. It's not that easy to decipher intent, or tell the difference between good and bad intentions. Manipulation, after all, is an exercise in personal salesmanship—the first objective is to entice or engage another in the force of one's personality. The end purpose is to make one's character believable, cunning, or superior enough to "sell" anything. The motive is either "sold" as well or convincingly disguised. So it's harder to tell when they lie, cheat, and treat you poorly—and then, more often than not, make it seem like your own fault.

For that reason, few beings are more treacherous than a bad person with good people skills.

A crafty manipulator knows how to run the "long con." They rarely expose themselves at the outset of a relationship and keep their aims close to the vest. They painstakingly go through the steps of building trust, encouraging frankness on your part about your hopes, dreams, challenges, and vulnerabilities. They listen and respond to your sentiments and affections with what looks like real concern and rapt interest. In early conversations they display undivided attention, seem to agree with your every statement, and pay you enthusiastic compliments or stroke your ego. They may not even be doing this consciously; they just know the patterns that have worked in the past with people to get their way.

What's troublesome is how positive those initial exchanges can be, just as they are in successful relationships. These moments reinforce our egos—especially if they're bruised. It feels good to interact with someone who appears unselfish and considerate. It can be nearly impossible to see how they're looking for weaknesses and vulnerabilities they can exploit to their advantage. Manipulators are routinely charismatic when they want to be—that's their first trick in selling people on themselves.

Then experienced manipulators test your soft spots, foibles, and Achilles' heels in small increments, a little at a time. An insult here, a cutting remark there, a joke that hits too close to home. Because of this deliberate and patient plan, it's a process you simply can't see when it's happening. It's almost impossible to catch until they've woven themselves into your life and secured their bonds. Extricating ourselves from these ties can be hard to pull off, even after you've discovered their motives.

But the small signs can be apparent early in a relationship. They may try to "out-victim" you by emphasizing their troubles over yours. They may speak about actions they'll take but never actually execute them. They may note your weak spots—appearance, confidence, social awkwardness—and make curt or dismissive comments about them.

That's why it's important to know and remember one proven, established fact: *psychological manipulation is abuse.* And it's something you must learn to recognize and defend against.

It's not a "sticking point" to work through. It's not something people "don't mean to do." It's not something "you deserve because you acted so poorly." It's not a minor "hang-up" to work through, as one would with different tastes, styles, or ticks. There is never a justification for it, and as Günner Karakurt determined in a study, it's not something limited to certain genders, sexes, ages, or roles. It's a protracted, very sustainable form of harm and mistreatment, and can be administered and experienced by anybody.

Again, it's never easy to ferret out the actions of an emotional abuser, especially when they lurk underneath the surface of an apparently stable relationship, and are sometimes subject to complicated perceptions. But there are common types of emotional manipulation that we can recognize through certain red flags or signs. Just because someone doesn't outright insult you, or hit you, doesn't mean abuse is not occurring. Don't make that mistake.

Belittling. Disapproval doesn't necessarily come in the direct form we recognize. It's often couched in cutting remarks, or disguised as a humorous or sarcastic quip—a quick line about your appearance, a statement you made, or something you like. But like more straightforward verbal attacks, they're intended to list your flaws and make you feel foolish. In a sense, manipulation is clever because it makes the manipulated assume all fault without the manipulator being in the spotlight. If you complain about them, the manipulator will flip the situation by claiming you're overly sensitive and critical. The long-term intention is to make you easier to control by making you feel inferior.

Belittling can be couched in kindness or concern just as easily. Someone might express that you "actually look presentable today," or relieve you of a responsibility because it's "too hard for someone like you," or dismiss a point you make because you "don't usually understand how things really work." All these miniature aggressions are intended to set up their position of power, which is never a benchmark for a successful relationship.

Never accepting fault. To prop up their domination, a serial manipulator will weave an improbable, ridiculous lie—or, if you prefer, an "alternate truth"—and will do so with absolute conviction and confidence. If their story involves a problem, they'll never accept any fault, blame, or responsibility. Normally, the story will miraculously shift in a way that, indeed, the manipulated is at fault.

Frequently, their machinations and lies will be so preposterous that even the abused might find them suspect. But the manipulator works so hard to talk out a complicated scenario, inventing detail after detail and painting themselves as a thwarted savior or innocent victim. If the smokescreen doesn't throw you off, the sheer amount of effort they use might be so exhausting that you'll drop the subject. Either result is a victory for the abuser, who just wants the conflict to stop.

For example, imagine you arrive at work to find you've missed an important meeting because the time was changed. Your workplace tried to call you about it, but talked to your roommate and gave them a message, which you never got. Then, instead of accepting responsibility for not giving you the message, they cast themselves as the victim by blaming you for getting home late, thereby ruining the dinner they prepared for you.

Guilt tripping. Manipulators will maintain a scorecard of everything they've done for you in an effort to make you feel in constant debt to them. If you refuse to go along with it, they'll claim you don't appreciate them, or are being mean or insensitive. They may keep a mental tally of the times they've driven you to work, or been "forced" to hang out with your friends they proclaim not to like. On a more intimate level they may ask you to do something because "you would if you loved me." These are all attempts at martyrdom, but in truth exhibit their selfishness.

The more dramatic they act, the worse the problem. In the end, they've worked you into a corner where you have no choice but to say yes to their demands; otherwise, you are a terrible person whom no one can love.

Angry outbursts. Many of us are conflict-averse, and manipulators jump on that quality to establish power and direct attention to themselves. They might angrily interrupt a casual conversation between you and someone else if it's heading in a direction the abuser doesn't like (or if it temporarily excludes them). Their intent is to make you accede to their attitude in order to "keep the peace."

Having disrupted the normality, they've accomplished their conquest in a scenario that didn't originally have a win/loss element. In private situations where no outsiders are there to see what transpires, an abuser can feel freer to let their anger be even more unfiltered and hurtful. Screaming, beating on tabletops, forceful hand gestures, and *especially* aggressive physical contact are vital warning signs that you need to exit a situation. It's unlikely you'll bring that issue up again if only to avoid that sort of situation again.

Disengagement. On the other end of angry eruptions are detachment and stonewalling. These can be tricky to spot because there's no overt sign of hostility—just a refusal to make any effort to connect, or simply denying anybody else's viewpoints or feelings. In short, they just don't try. They might retire to another room in the house when confronted with a subject they find hard to discuss. They may physically withdraw from your presence and note their lack of interest. They may go days without speaking a word after you "activate" a trigger you didn't know about.

While this tactic can also be taken as a trait of a recessive or shy personality, emotional manipulators use it to extricate themselves from their end of a relationship, often as skillfully as their more obviously harmful ways. There's no way for this relationship to continue until the manipulated breaks and first apologizes.

Manipulation Doesn't Happen in a Vacuum

This could be a dangerous statement, because it could be interpreted that the victim of an abusive situation bears some responsibility. That's entirely untrue. Victims can't control the thought patterns, actions, or statements of their abusers. Especially since an aim of the manipulator is to make instill a sense of guilt in others, it's important for their victims to understand they are *not* accountable for their abuser's decision to abuse.

That statement means that a manipulator will seek emotional settings that are conducive to their needs for power and control, and sometimes this includes people with certain behavioral patterns.

Although anyone can fall prey to them, an emotional manipulator's most typical targets are more open, accepting, easy-going, and sympathetic—people who:

- Often sacrifice their own well-being for the sake of others
- Crave acceptance and approval
- Are more likely to "give in" in a conflict or confrontation
- Have weak boundaries and can't say no
- Suffer from self-esteem issues

While identifying the common tactics of a manipulator is 95% of the battle, being honest about your own qualities can help you discern the reality of an abusive setup. You don't have to sacrifice your positive attributes as a result of an abusive situation—but knowing how those who aren't so positive can maneuver them is a plank in our survival. That's where the important act of setting boundaries comes in.

Setting Emotional Boundaries

That people don't always behave as we'd like is a hard lesson to learn in all relationships. Seeing apathy, carelessness, or a lack of respect for others' feelings is a great source of stress and unhappiness. Trying to modify others to act and feel in ways we prefer is an exhausting and futile exercise.

All we *can* do is adjust ourselves and what we accept from others. We demonstrate our capacity for love, communication, support, and inspiration as best we can, in ways we hope can be perceived. In others, we seek affirmation, or at least recognition, of our best efforts. In rare cases, we may find those whose ideals closely duplicate our own. But ultimately, other people do what they're going to do, and we either accept them for who they are or walk away from them.

However, there's an element of relationships that you have more control over than you may think. It's a healthy kind of control that respects your values and feelings, and reinforces your balanced relations with others. That element is *setting and keeping emotional boundaries*.

This doesn't mean devising a list of rules that other people must live up to, or risk losing your friendship. Neither does it mean erecting a wall around your emotions or feelings in over-protection. What boundaries *do* mean is making standards for in caring for yourself, in ways that reflect your core values and personal priorities. They keep you from being swamped by others' demands, and help foster more balanced relationships with the potential for true intimacy.

Boundaries in healthy relationships are strong and scrupled, but flexible enough to respond to altered circumstances and each party's own uniqueness. They support each member's efforts to live full lives, while developing legitimate respect, trust, and support over a long period of time. Setting up boundaries is an introspective and practical process, and occasionally people will tell you that your boundaries are wrong. They might be right; but subjective boundaries also exist.

Define your limits. Be honest with yourself about the point where others' behavior crosses your personal lines for acceptance and safety. What subjects do you need to be treated carefully, no matter how objectively silly they might sound? At what level does someone's voice go from concern to anger? What makes you comfortable, and what makes you anxious?

Monitor your feelings. "Trusting your gut" is certainly a key thing to do when confronted with an immediate situation. But pay close attention to how you're reacting in social or low-pressure circumstances as well. If a conversation's taking a turn that makes you uncomfortable, mark that point and ask yourself what could be causing your stress. Being self-aware in itself isn't a sign of narcissism or selfishness—it's a basic survival mechanism.

Set a communication plan. Very few of us talk or act the same way with every single person we know (if we do, that's probably a problem). But in close relationships, at some point the need to discuss our boundaries will arise, and you should make a plan in advance on how to communicate your feelings. Being direct is always the preference, but the definition of our relationship is important in figuring out how to express that directness. In personal relationships, we might feel free to speak freely and ruminate. In professional or complicated situations, we may need to be level and determined.

Signs of Unhealthy Boundaries

Keeping up a sense of self-awareness, as mentioned, is a key part of relationship health. Being truthful about the effectiveness of our internal boundaries—and taking proactive, corrective measures when they fall short—is crucial to this honesty. It also goes a very long way in protecting one's self against the operations of emotional manipulators.

When taking such personal inventory, it's vital to recognize indications that our emotional boundaries need some adjustments:

- Feeling that people take advantage of you and your emotions for their own gains
- Constantly finding yourself "saving" people close to you and fixing their problems
- Claiming that you "hate drama," but always finding yourself in the middle of it (family arguments, extraordinarily complicated romantic situations, work gossip)
- Defending yourself for things that aren't your fault (traffic jams making you late, people projecting opinions or feelings that you never had or shared)
- Saying yes to things you'd rather not do simply to evade conflict or guilt (making big loans to family members who don't pay back, cancelling social plans for a dramatically needy friend or partner)
- Feeling resentful because you do more for others than they do for you

- Repressing your emotions and frustrations because you're afraid to set family boundaries
- Expecting that people closest to you should "just know" when they've upset you

Recognizing Boundary Violations

Even if we know and set our emotional boundaries, we may overlook them in practice with others, or not always recognize when our boundaries are being trespassed. Since emotional manipulators thrive on blurring those boundaries and resetting them to reflect their own interests, developing a keener sense of when those trespasses happen is extremely useful.

It's easier to notice verbal violations, for obvious reasons. Any effort to invalidate or disparage your characters or emotions should be evaluated in relation to your boundaries. These include someone not allowing you to speak or be heard by silencing or talking over you, screaming, making derogatory statements about your integrity, or even flat-out gossiping about you in plain sight.

Violations of your psychological and emotional boundaries can be more difficult to spot and harder to quantify. They could include:

- Preying on your self-esteem
- Using things you've said to them in confidence against you
- Lying
- Criticizing, demeaning, and judging
- Making fun of you or your thoughts, feelings, and beliefs
- Making you feel guilty or responsible
- Demanding your time and energy
- Shaming and embarrassing
- Bullying
- Claiming their thoughts and beliefs are superior to yours

While defining and setting up boundaries is the important pivot point in any relationship, maintaining them is equally essential. Psychologist Dana Gionta identified two key feelings that should be red flags that we're letting go of our boundaries:

Discomfort. "When someone acts in a way that makes you feel uncontrollable, that's a cue to us they may be violating or crossing a boundary." Discomfort can arise from triggers about past issues or traumas, someone communicating in an overly frantic or antagonistic way, or being in an unexpected or unsafe situation. It can also simply arise from being put in a position where you feel interpersonal tension.

Resentment. This usually comes from "being taken advantage of, or not being appreciated." We feel guilty, or that someone else is imposing their expectations on us. Resentment can arise when we're asked to fix an ongoing series of crises, or get left out of important work decisions after habitually working overtime, or simply don't get anything back from what we give.

Gionta recommends gauging our feelings on a scale from one to ten, and sounding the alarm if one feels our intensity goes higher than six. When that happens, she suggests asking what's causing the feelings, and what about the situation is bothering you.

Frequently, the root impetuses are fear, guilt, and self-doubt. We fear others' responses when we set and keep our boundaries. We feel guilty if we speak up or say no. And we doubt that we even deserve to have boundaries in the first place.

What we have to remember is that boundaries are key signs of a healthy relationship, and vital steps toward self-respect. You're the exclusive owner of your own feelings, and as their protector, you have full permission to set and preserve your emotional boundaries.

But knowing where you stand is a necessary measure in deciding your boundaries. Identify your limits: physical, emotional, mental, and spiritual. Concentrate on what you can tolerate and what you can't accept. "Those feelings help us identify what our limits are," Gionta says.

When instituting boundaries, it's critical to be aware of the values and roles that were imposed upon us in growing up. For example, a person who grew up with an ill parent might have had to be a caretaker for much of their youth—which could cause them to ignore their own needs. Living with a family who frequently fought, verbally or physically, could have laid the groundwork for one's approach to confrontation.

Take time to consider your present social circle and close friendships. Think about whether your give-and-take is healthy, and whether the relationships are truly reciprocal. If you notice a certain behavioral strain or commonality with your friends (or with yourself), address it in your investigation whether good or bad—it could help detect further clues about your emotional realities.

Finally, examine how your daily environment outside of relationships could be impacting your health. Your work environment is a good place to start. For example, if your work day is supposed to be eight hours, but your coworkers regularly stay at least 10 or 11, is there an unspoken mandate that you're supposed to go "above and beyond"? How does your office cope with sudden emergencies or long-term conflicts?

Keeping boundaries intact is a solo exercise—it springs from your own personal observations and experience. It can be challenging, especially if somebody feels they're the only one trying to maintain boundaries. But it's a regular way to tend to our feelings and needs, and a good mechanism to remind ourselves how we need to honor them.

Summary Guide

Chapter 1. Our Volatile Emotions

Our emotions exist for the very specific reason of keeping us alive, but that sometimes doesn't translate so well into the modern era.

Chapter 2. Emotional Triggers

Most of the time, what we are affected by emotionally is unrelated to what is happening. It is simply an external trigger for an internal emotional need that is unfulfilled or threatened.

Chapter 3. The Emotional Immune System

Self-esteem has frequently been called the emotional immune system because you will be far more resilient with it than without. It is important to increase self-worth, let go of perfectionism, and keep expectations rooted in reality.

Chapter 4. Defining the Emotional Spectrum

Even thought you think it might be the answer, emotional suppression is unhealthy and just makes things worse. Feel your emotions, and in fact, try to feel as many emotions as possible and put accurate names to them to help with your processing and coping.

Chapter 5. Recognition, Regulation, and Response

Feel your emotions, but recognize them, regulate them with exercises and analyzing the factors involved, and respond to them rather than react. This is the best way to maintain emotional resilience.

Chapter 6. The Heat of the Moment

Emotional regulation is about changing the narrative, improving your negative self-talk, and indeed changing the type of story you are used to telling.

Chapter 7. Perspective

The Buddhist concept of detachment is not about apathy, it's about not growing dependent on anything external for your emotional satisfaction because it is all actually created in your own head. Stoic philosophy is similar, in that emotions are man-made and all events are neutral - we just assign meaning to them, and this is what we can control.

Chapter 8. Safeguarding Tactics

These tactics keep your mind clear, and keep you paying attention to how your emotional states are affected. Journaling, making two distinctly different types of lists, and practicing gratitude are valuable for providing perspective.

Chapter 9. Preventative Care is the Best Care

Try to proactively combat the negative bias your brain constructs for you by creating anticipation, savoring more, and looking at the small victories in life.

Chapter 10. Emotional Self-Defense

You might not be the reason for your lack of self-esteem or emotional resiliency. The first step is to recognize if you are being manipulated, and then understand how boundaries should be set according to your discomfort and resentment.

Made in the USA
Middletown, DE
13 October 2023

40734770R00126